AMERICAN IMPERIALISM
Viewpoints of United States
Foreign Policy, 1898-1941

WAR IN CHINA

America's Role in the Far East

Varian Fry

71643

ARNO PRESS & THE NEW YORK TIMES

New York ★ 1970

951
F947w

Collection Created and Selected
by
CHARLES GREGG OF GREGG PRESS

Reprinted by permission of the Foreign Policy Association, Incorporated
Reprinted from a copy in The Hoover Institution Library

Library of Congress Catalog Card Number: 76-111741
ISBN 0-405-02021-X

ISBN for complete set: 0-405-02000-7

Reprint Edition 1970 by Arno Press Inc.
Manufactured in the United States of America

WAR IN CHINA

America's Role in The Far East

VARIAN FRY

With maps and charts by
HENRY ADAMS GRANT

THE FOREIGN POLICY ASSOCIATION

CONTENTS

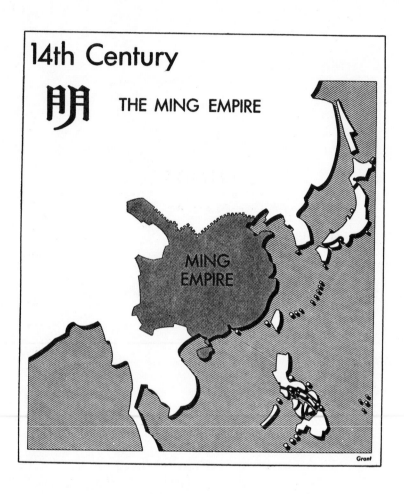

14th Century

朋 THE MING EMPIRE

MING EMPIRE

Grant

I. The Manchus Lose an Empire

If someone should ask you when China first began to have regular dealings with the western world, ten to one you'd think of the clipper ships and say, "Oh, about a hundred years ago, I guess."

Well, you'd be wrong. As early as the fourth century B.C. the ancient Greeks were receiving raw silk from China and weaving it into a luxurious and immensely expensive cloth. And from that time until the Turks captured Constantinople, in 1453, there was a steady flow of goods from China to the West, and a steady flow of goods back from Europe to China.

Though this trade persisted and, at times, even flourished, it had very little effect on China's life and civilization—much less influence, in fact, than it had on the West. But when the first European sailors of modern times showed up at the port of Canton, in southern China, in 1516 (just three years before Magellan set out on his famous trip around the world), they started a chain of events which ultimately affected Chinese history profoundly.

THE MING EMPIRE

In those far-away days China was ruled by a royal dynasty called the Mings. You may have heard their name used to describe porcelain and "china" made during their long reign. The Mings were a Chinese dynasty, and the kingdom they ruled over was what is now called "China proper." It did not include any of the outlying states, like Sinkiang (shin-djiong) or "Chinese Turkestan," Mongolia and Manchuria—though certain chieftains in those areas, as well as the rulers of Korea and several other states, paid regular tribute to the Ming Emperors.

7

At first the Mings were willing to let the Europeans travel and trade anywhere they liked in China. But after some unpleasant experiences with the western merchants, they decided they did not want them running all over their empire after all. So they refused to let them travel in China or enter any harbor but Canton. And they made strict rules about trade with the Europeans even there.

The Mings ruled China for nearly 300 years. And then, suddenly, a tribe of fierce warriors swept down from the north and drove them from their throne.

THE MANCHU EMPIRE

These northerners were the Manchus (man-chews). They were *not* Chinese. But they conquered China and Mongolia, Sinkiang and Tibet, adding them all to their own kingdom of Manchuria to form one vast Asiatic Empire. Not only that: they made Korea, Nepal, Bhutan, Burma and the various states of Indo-China vassal states of their great empire.

When the Manchus had established themselves at Peking (bay-ping), they opened all China to European trade (1685). But the European merchants abused the privilege so outrageously that the Manchus soon came to see the wisdom of the Mings' more cautious policy. Once again all the ports except Canton were closed, and at Canton new regulations were made which were even stricter than before (1717).

Under the Manchus' new laws, no barbarian, as the Chinese called the foreigners, could enter the city of Canton. The European merchants were met outside the city walls by Chinese merchants who had been appointed by the Emperor to deal with them. If the Europeans didn't care for the way these merchants did business, there was nothing for them to do but go home. They were never permitted to see any Chinese

8

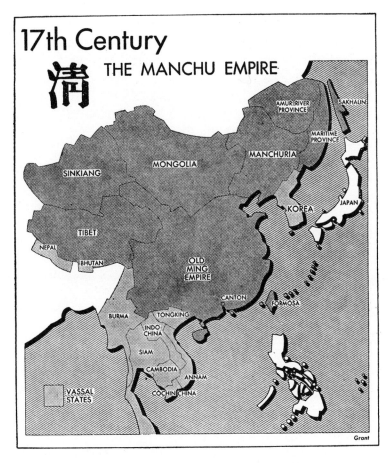

17th Century

龍 THE MANCHU EMPIRE

SAKHALIN

AMUR RIVER
PROVINCE

MARITIME
PROVINCE

MANCHURIA

MONGOLIA

SINKIANG

KOREA

JAPAN

TIBET

NEPAL

BHUTAN

OLD
MING
EMPIRE

CANTON

FORMOSA

BURMA

TONGKING

INDO-
CHINA

SIAM

CAMBODIA

ANNAM

VASSAL
STATES

COCHIN CHINA

Grant

officials, and if they had any complaints to make about the
way the Chinese merchants treated them, they had no one but
the merchants themselves to complain to.

This situation was very unsatisfactory to the foreigners, and
especially to the English, who made several attempts to change
it. But they got exactly nowhere.

9

THE OPIUM WAR

Then something happened which changed everything almost overnight. That something was the Opium War.

Dr. Fu Manchu and the movies have shown us so many Chinese opium dens that many people think opium smoking was invented by the Chinese. That's another wrong idea about China. The truth is that the Chinese first got opium from India. They used it as we do today, for medicine. But the Dutch merchants who had settled on the island of Formosa mixed it with tobacco and smoked it, and the Chinese apparently learned to smoke it from them. By 1800 the English were doing a big business selling opium to the Chinese. The trade was forbidden by Chinese law, but this did not prevent the merchants of the West from continuing to profit from it.

In 1839 the Manchu government decided to stamp out the opium trade once and for all. They appointed a man named Lin as High Commissioner to end the opium traffic, and Commissioner Lin immediately ordered all the merchants at Canton to surrender their opium to him.

The British say that the war which followed was not fought to defend their right to sell opium to the Chinese, but to compel the Manchu government to respect the rights of all foreigners and treat the foreign merchants fairly. Whether this is true or not, we should at least remember that back of the opium issue there was a long controversy between the Chinese and the foreigners as to how to carry on business, administer "justice," and handle diplomatic relations between China and the government officials who were representing the foreign traders.

Well, the English won the war (1840-42), and when they had won it they made the Manchu Emperor's representatives sign a treaty which not only changed the status of foreign merchants in China, but set in motion a process which gradually undermined the foundations of Chinese society, drove the Manchus from their throne, and left China divided and disorganized for many years.

THE FIRST TREATY SETTLEMENT

In the treaty the Emperor's representatives ceded to England the island of Hongkong and agreed to let British merchants enter Canton and four other Chinese ports (including Shanghai). They also promised not to charge more than 5 per cent duty on exports or imports. And, in some "General Regulations" issued shortly afterward, they gave up their right to try British subjects who were charged with committing crimes on Chinese territory: in future, these regulations provided, all such wrongdoers would be tried by the British consuls in China. This arrangement, which is known as "extraterritoriality," was soon extended to other nations. It has developed so far since 1843 that many western countries, including the United States, now have their own courts, their own police forces, even their own gunboats, in China.

Of course, neither we nor any other nation would have gone to the considerable expense and trouble of maintaining courts, police forces, marines and gunboats in China if it had not been necessary for us to do so. The simple truth is that without some such protection Westerners would not have been safe in China, such was the turbulence and disorder which prevailed in that country during the latter years of the Manchu Empire and the early years of the republic which succeeded it. In fact, as we shall see, Westerners were not always safe in China even *with* their courts and marines and gunboats. But while these extraterritorial rights helped to provide the foreigners in China with some much-needed assurance against unjust treatment and even sudden and violent death, they also served to undermine still further the already rapidly declining authority of the Chinese government.

The treaty of 1842, which the Chinese officials concluded with the British, was the signal for a series of wars and treaties in which the Manchus gradually lost or signed away more than half their empire and many of the rights which every nation considers essential to its sovereignty, or independence.

THE MOST-FAVORED-NATION CLAUSE

Only experts in Far Eastern affairs need to know the year-by-year history of these wars and treaties. But there is one fact about the treaties everyone should know. As the Chinese officials signed treaties with one country after another, they included a paragraph known as a "most-favored-nation clause." In these clauses China promised to give to the country with which she was making the treaty the same rights and privileges she had granted or might grant in the future to the "most favored nation"—that is, the nation to which she had granted the most. In this way every country which made a treaty with China got all the rights and privileges any other country forced out of her. The United States has never fought a war with China, but, thanks to the most-favored-nation clauses in our treaties with her, we have gotten every privilege (except actual grants of land) which England or France or Russia has forced China to grant.

THE TAIPING REBELLION

Not long after the opium war the Manchus had a civil war on their hands. This war is known as the Taiping (tie-ping)

12

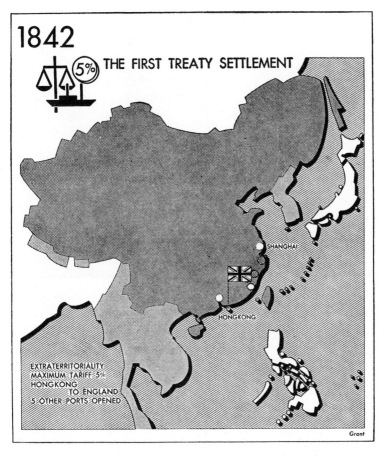

1842

5%

THE FIRST TREATY SETTLEMENT

SHANGHAI

HONGKONG

EXTRATERRITORIALITY
MAXIMUM TARIFF 5%
HONGKONG
        TO ENGLAND
5 OTHER PORTS OPENED

Grant

Rebellion. It was fifteen years (1850–65) before the Manchus
were able to re-establish their authority over the rebellious
provinces, and while they were occupied in putting the rebellion down, the English and the French took advantage of the
situation to get still more privileges. They fought a joint war
against the Manchus. And, of course, they won.

13

THE SECOND TREATY SETTLEMENT

As a result, new treaties were signed (1858–60). These treaties opened eleven more ports to foreign trade, allowed foreigners to travel anywhere they pleased in the Manchu Empire, pledged the Chinese authorities to protect Christian missionaries traveling or living in their country, legalized the sale of opium, and permitted western nations to maintain their diplomatic representatives at the Manchu capital, Peking. As before, other nations got the same rights without having to fight for them. Besides the general privileges, Great Britain also took a slice of the mainland back of Hongkong (called Kowloon), and Russia got the Maritime Province in which the great port of Vladivostok is now located.

THE DISMEMBERMENT OF THE MANCHU EMPIRE

From that time on, the power of the Manchus rapidly declined, and their empire was stolen from under their noses piece by piece. More ports were opened up. In many of the treaty ports one or more of the powers obtained "concessions" or districts over which they could exercise every bit as much authority as if those districts had been located within their own borders. France took Cochin China and Cambodia in 1862. Annam and Tongking became French "protectorates" in 1882. In 1885 Great Britain helped herself to Burma and made Nepal and Bhutan into British protectorates. In 1893 France enlarged her empire in Indo-China by annexing Annam outright. In 1895 Japan . . .

But with the mention of Japan we meet a newcomer to the company of imperialist powers in Asia, the one which now considers herself destined to drive the others out. Before we carry China's story any further, we shall have to go back

1858-60

THE SECOND TREATY SETTLEMENT

AMUR RIVER PROVINCE

MARITIME PROVINCE

PEKING
TIENTSIN

YANGTZE RIVER

KOWLOON

AMUR RIVER PROVINCE TO RUSSIA
MARITIME PROVINCE TO RUSSIA
KOWLOON TO ENGLAND

10 MORE PORTS OPENED
REPRESENTATIVES IN PEKING
FOREIGNERS PERMITTED TO TRAVEL
MISSIONARIES GRANTED PROTECTION
SALE OF OPIUM LEGALIZED

Grant

and tell the story of Japan from the time the West first knocked at her door.

II. Commodore Perry Rouses Japan

It was America which started Japan on the path of empire. For exactly ninety-nine years (1542-1641) European merchants had been allowed to enter the Island Kingdom and carry on their business there. But in 1641 all but a handful of Dutch traders were turned out, and from that time until Commodore Perry sailed into Yedo Bay, in 1853, Japan was more completely isolated from the world than China had ever been.

When American trading ships began to sail the China Sea, a year after the Revolution, and American whaling vessels began to comb the north Pacific a few decades later, storms would sometimes drive them off their course and wreck them on the rocky coasts of Japan. As there was no regular service to Japan, the shipwrecked sailors often found it very difficult to get home again. Nor were the Japanese always very kindly hosts: some of the returning sailors told stories of cruelty and mistreatment fit to make your hair stand on end. And at least part of what they said seems to have been true.

THE PERRY MISSION

Around the middle of the last century, President Millard Fillmore decided to put an end to this state of affairs. Selecting Commodore Matthew Calbraith Perry of the United States Navy to be his representative, he sent him to Japan with four warships, two of them driven by steam. Besides a letter of introduction to the Japanese Mikado, Commodore Perry took with him a number of presents, including some of the latest inventions of the time, a telegraph set and a working model of a steam locomotive, complete with cars and track. His instructions were to get a treaty guaranteeing the safety of

16

American sailors shipwrecked near Japan. But the treaty he obtained was a mere incident compared to the influence his presents had on the development of Japanese civilization.

JAPAN IN 1853

What Perry found in Japan was a primitive feudal society. The Emperor lived in a palace in the mountains, and took almost no part in the business of governing the country. The real ruler was the "Shogun" (show-gun), a kind of hereditary political boss whose job had grown to be much more important than the Emperor's. From his court at Tokyo, this official attempted to govern the unruly nobles in the provinces, and what central power there was in Japan was gathered in his hands. But, like the barons of mediaeval Europe, the Japanese nobles spent most of their time fighting one another. Each noble, or "daimyo" (die-me-oh, a title which means "Great Name"), had his own private army, equipped with bows and arrows, and the poor Shogun had about as much trouble keeping order as the kings of Europe in the Middle Ages.

If, politically, Japan was a feudal society in 1853, industrially it was a handicrafts society. When Perry sailed up Yedo Bay with his "black ships," his telegraph set, his toy train, and his letter of introduction to the Emperor, there wasn't a factory of the modern sort in all Japan; Perry's own warships were the first steam vessels the Japanese had ever seen; and his model train was as much of a novelty to them as a machine gun would have been to a crusader. In other words, Japan was at about the stage of industrial development Western Europe had reached when Johannes Gutenberg began to think of printing books with movable type, just four hundred years before.

Sixty years later Japan was one of the leading industrial powers of the world.

JAPAN'S RISE TO POWER

The story of this amazing development is the story of a decentralized, feudal society turning itself into a centralized, "national" state in about twenty-five years—a growth it took Europe three hundred years and more to achieve. And then it is the story of the newly nationalized state starting from scratch and, in many respects, catching up with the industrial giants of the West in one generation.

Even before Commodore Perry "loudly knocked at their door," and "roused them from their century-long slumber," the Japanese nobles had been aware of what was happening to the Manchu Empire. As they watched England, France and Russia helping themselves to slice after slice of the Manchus' territory and extracting concession after concession from China's distracted rulers, the Japanese nobles decided that they were not going to have the same tricks played on them.

But the Shogun already had the process well on its way. After Perry's visit, he had signed treaties not only with the United States but also with Great Britain, Russia and the Netherlands. And in them he had granted many of the privileges which the Manchus had granted in China.

Therefore the nobles' first step was to overthrow the Shogun. Nor was that difficult to do. In signing treaties with the western powers, that official had run head-on into a fire of anti-foreign feeling, and it was an easy matter for the nobles to fan the flames until they drove the Shogun out. A short time before, a new Emperor had ascended the throne; he became the first in over 250 years really to rule Japan.

18

THE ERA OF MEIJI

The Japanese call the period of this Emperor's reign (1867 to 1912) the "era of Meiji" (mage-ee)—the "Enlightened Rule." In rapid succession the government was centralized, feudalism was all but destroyed, certain democratic institutions were introduced, a modern army was established, a modern navy begun, the Shogun's "unequal" treaties with the western powers were thrown off, and many of the methods of modern industry were imported from the West. Like the Russians today, the Japanese sent students to Europe and America to study and observe western industrial methods and then go back home to put their newly gained knowledge to use. And, like the Russians again, they hired European and American experts to go to Japan and help build railroads and factories, install telegraph and telephone systems, and in a thousand ways make their country over.

Unlike the Russians, however, the Japanese worked without a plan, and so some of their new industries developed much faster than others, agriculture failed to keep pace with industry, and in many branches of Japanese economy feudalistic habits lingered on long after they had ceased to be useful. Many of Japan's troubles today come from this uneven development. Yet it is probably fair to say that by the end of the Meiji era, thanks to the farsightedness of her feudal nobles, Japan was beginning to compete on almost equal terms with the countries of Europe and America.

JAPAN TAKES THE WAR PATH

But she was doing more than that: spurred on by the imperialistic ambitions of her governing class, the pressure of her rapidly expanding population, and the necessity of finding

19

markets and sources of raw materials for her new and growing industries, she was slowly but surely transforming herself into the mistress of Eastern Asia.

As early as 1858 Lord Hotta, one of the nobles at the court, had advised the Emperor to prepare for the day when Japan should rule the world. "The object should always be . . . securing hegemony over all nations," he had said. It was a tempting goal, and some of the members of Japan's feudal military caste adopted it with a whoop. Today there is in Japan an influential group which solemnly and devoutly believes that their country is destined to save the world by conquering it.

There are also some Japanese who are simply self-seeking imperialists, bent on conquest for the homely purpose of acquiring new markets, new agricultural land, new sources of raw materials, new homes for an expanding population. And there are still others—perhaps many others—who would like their country to renounce conquest altogether and live in peace with its neighbors and the world. But the fanatical crusading group, the group which believes that "the salvation of the entire human race is the mission of our Empire," as one of them puts it, the group which will root for war no matter what it costs or where it leads—this group is the one which has led the others on. You can't hope to understand Japan's recent acts unless you keep the program of this group constantly in mind.

The first faltering step toward realizing that program was taken in 1874, when, after a long-drawn-out dispute and a threat of force, Japan took the Liuchu (lee-oo-chew) islands from China. The Liuchus, however, were relatively unimportant, and it was not until 1894 that the Empire of the Rising Sun was ready for a major war of conquest.

20

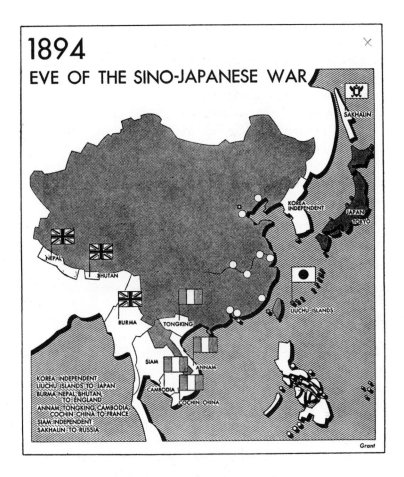

1894

EVE OF THE SINO-JAPANESE WAR

X

SAKHALIN

KOREA
INDEPENDENT

JAPAN
TOKYO

NEPAL

BHUTAN

LIUCHU ISLANDS

BURMA

TONGKING

SIAM

ANNAM

CAMBODIA

COCHIN CHINA

KOREA INDEPENDENT
LIUCHU ISLANDS TO JAPAN
BURMA, NEPAL, BHUTAN,
    TO ENGLAND
ANNAM, TONGKING, CAMBODIA,
    COCHIN CHINA TO FRANCE
SIAM INDEPENDENT
SAKHALIN TO RUSSIA

Grant

X THE SINO-JAPANESE WAR

In that year Japan picked a fight with China over the peninsula of Korea, one of the Manchus' vassal states. To the
surprise of the rest of the world, which had not yet realized
how strong Japan had become, she won, and in 1895 she signed

a treaty with the Manchus in which they acknowledged the independence of Korea and handed over to Japan, lock, stock and barrel, the large island of Formosa, the tiny Pescadores Islands near by, and the Liaotung (lee-ah-oh-doong) Peninsula at the southern end of Manchuria.

Then three of the western powers did something which made the Japanese hopping mad. Within a week after the treaty between Japan and China was signed, Russia, Germany and France intervened and forced Japan to give the Liaotung Peninsula back to the Manchus. Reluctantly the Japanese agreed. But they deeply resented the interference.

MORE GRABS

Their resentment flared into anger when they saw the very same powers turn around and demand "payment" from the Manchus for the "service" they had rendered them. France asked and received another part of Indo-China, and Russia got permission to build a railroad across northern Manchuria. Three years later Germany took Kiaochow (gee-ah-oh-joe) in the province of Shantung (shahn-doong), and Russia took Kwantung (gwahn-doong), the tip of the very peninsula she had forced Japan to "give back" to the Manchus.

To be sure, these later transfers of territory were not outright grants but "leaseholds." That is, China agreed to rent the cities and surrounding countryside for a period of 99 years, during which time the western powers were to pay rent just as people pay rent for apartments and houses in American cities. But can you imagine the United States renting San Francisco to Japan? Well, China was no more eager to rent her cities to foreign countries than we should be to rent ours. But the western powers threatened to use their navies if

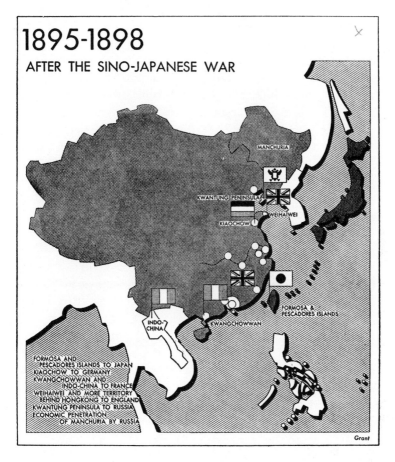

1895-1898

AFTER THE SINO-JAPANESE WAR

MANCHURIA

KWANTUNG PENINSULA

WEIHAIWEI

KIAOCHOW

FORMOSA &
PESCADORES ISLANDS

INDO-
CHINA

KWANGCHOWWAN

FORMOSA AND
PESCADORES ISLANDS TO JAPAN
KIAOCHOW TO GERMANY
KWANGCHOWWAN AND
INDO-CHINA TO FRANCE
WEIHAIWEI AND MORE TERRITORY
BEHIND HONGKONG TO ENGLAND
KWANTUNG PENINSULA TO RUSSIA
ECONOMIC PENETRATION
OF MANCHURIA BY RUSSIA

Grant

China refused to give them the leases they wanted, and,
as she was too weak to resist, China had to do as she was
ordered.

Nor was it only Russia and Germany who stuck pistols in
China's back and made her sign on the dotted line. Britain used
the same methods to get a long-term lease on another piece of

the mainland back of Hongkong, as well as on Weihaiwei (way-high-way), a port in Shantung. And France extracted a lease on Kwangchowwan (gwong-joe-wahn), far to the south.

This undignified scramble for "leaseholds," special privileges, and "spheres of influence" on the mainland of Asia had two results: it made the Japanese decide that they would make themselves strong enough to throw all the western nations out of Asia. And it led the United States to proclaim the famous doctrine of the "Open Door."

III. We Hold the Door Open

So far we have not heard much about the United States in China. The reason is that, unlike the leading nations of Europe, the United States played no very important role there before the end of the nineteenth century. Our China trade began in 1784, and to the people of New England it was for a time a vital source of livelihood. But in those early days we had no navy worthy of the name, and so our government could do little or nothing but let our traders fend for themselves, whatever the consequences. We therefore left it to the European powers to force China to give them rights and privileges. And, thanks to the most-favored-nation clauses in our treaties with the Manchus, we got everything the others got except actual transfers of territory.

But by 1898 it was a different story. In that year we fought a war with Spain, and when we had beaten the Spaniards we made them sell us the Philippine Islands. Now the Philippine Islands are as much a part of Asia as the islands of Japan, and the possession of them put us in the class of Asiatic powers

24

with one stroke of the pen. Since the day the Stars and Stripes were first run up on the flagpoles of Manila, we have become more and more deeply involved in the politics of Asia. For from that time on we have had not only a growing trade with Asia to protect but also a large and populous Asiatic colony.

JOHN HAY AND THE "OPEN DOOR"

By 1898 the scramble for spheres of political influence and control in China and the western Pacific had begun to alarm the powers of the world, and not the least alarmed was the United States. With the single exception of the Philippines, we had taken no part in that scramble, and it had begun to look as though we might soon be squeezed out of Asia altogether. In their treaties with us, as in their treaties with the other western nations, the Chinese had agreed not to charge more than 5 per cent duty on exports or imports passing through *their* ports. But now Russia, Germany, France and England were taking more and more of the Manchus' land away from them. Suppose the whole of the Manchu Empire should be divided up among the European powers. What then? Wouldn't American business men find themselves shut out by the very same tariff walls those nations were erecting back home?

At least there was no *guarantee* that they wouldn't.

That was the worry which confronted John Hay when President McKinley appointed him Secretary of State in 1898. In the hope of getting the great powers to commit themselves not to discriminate against American business men in the ports they leased and the areas they controlled in China, Hay wrote letters asking them to agree to treat all business men in China alike (1899).

Hay didn't have much success with his letters. Though

25

Britain had herself suggested the idea to him a year before, she reserved her right to do as she pleased in Hongkong and Kowloon, and she and the other countries only agreed to adopt Hay's policy if all the rest did too. And, as Russia never gave a satisfactory reply, no one was really bound by the letters. But Hay pretended that they were. He announced that, as all the nations he had written to had accepted the principles he had outlined in his letters, those principles had become "final and definitive."

At the time, this policy of the "Open Door," as it was called, said nothing about maintaining the "territorial and administrative integrity" of China: it was intended merely to protect *commercial* interests there. After the "Boxer Rebellion," Hay tried to expand the "Open Door" policy to include a guarantee of China's territory. But it was not until the Washington Conference of 1921–22 that the great powers finally agreed to stop dividing China up. And at least one of them—Japan—has broken her agreement since.

THE BOXER REBELLION

While England, France, Germany and Russia were using their gunboats to grab some of China's best ports, and Secretary Hay was writing his letters, the Chinese people were growing more and more incensed at the way the western nations were carving their country up. They were also troubled and puzzled by the disastrous effect the impact of the West was having on their ancient civilization. Christian missionaries were spreading the doctrine of a strange new faith which challenged age-old Chinese customs and beliefs. The influx of western factory-made goods was throwing Chinese artisans out of work. The costly wars with the foreigners were burdening

26

them with taxes. No wonder they resented the "barbarians" and did what they could to drive them out.

The actual ruler of China at that time was the Dowager Empress Tzu Hsi (dzeu-she). As fierce as any of her Manchu ancestors, she was known to her subjects as the "old tiger." Since many of the treaties with the West had been signed during her reign, Tzu Hsi had good reason to fear that the resentment against the foreigners would center on her. In the hope of shunting it off, she secretly encouraged anti-foreign outbreaks. When the Boxer Rebellion shocked the world, in the summer of 1900, Tzu Hsi was widely suspected of having connived at it.

We call this uprising the "Boxer Rebellion" because it was led by a secret society called the "Fists of Righteous Harmony," a name which English and American residents in China promptly translated into "Boxers." After killing nearly 250 foreigners, among them more than 50 children, the "Boxers" besieged the legations in Peking, where all the foreigners in the city, and most of the hated Christian Chinese, had taken refuge when the rebellion first broke out. As no word came from the legations for over a month, governments and people alike believed that every last man, woman and child who had fled to them had been slaughtered.

Finally the American Minister got through a cable appealing for help. By that time an international army was already fighting its way to Peking from the coast. But it was another month before the imprisoned foreigners, weak from lack of food and white with terror, were rescued.

Just before the relief expedition entered Peking, Tzu Hsi, badly frightened, disguised herself as an old peasant woman and fled. When the foreign forces got to Peking, they put the "old tiger" back on her throne, but they also made her pay. In

27

the settlement, China had to give a huge indemnity for the lives and property lost, agree to punish the rebels, and grant the foreign powers zones in Peking where they could have their own soldiers or marines to protect their legations from similar attacks in the future.

THE "OPEN DOOR" POLICY EXPANDS

If these terms did not infringe on China's "territorial and administrative integrity," the man China could thank was Secretary Hay. Throughout the disturbances he had held the other nations back, and when peace was restored it was he who persuaded them to send the greater part of their armies home. Without his efforts, too, the indemnities would have been even larger than they were, and the great powers would have demanded new concessions, privileges, and spheres of political control like the many they had obtained in the past. Hay openly asked them all to state that they would respect China's independence and territorial integrity, and, since the invitation was public, they couldn't very well refuse. But, although they agreed, they agreed with reservations. Great Britain was beginning to think of establishing a "sphere of influence" in Tibet, a desire she gratified later (1904). Russia wanted not only Manchuria but Mongolia: Outer Mongolia has actually become a Russian "sphere" since. France would gladly have taken further chunks of the Manchu Empire if and when she saw a chance. And Germany, which had started late, and was therefore a long way behind the others in the game of grab, was every bit as eager to enrich herself at China's expense as they were. Even Italy was beginning to look China-ward. The last thing they wanted was to make promises that would prevent them from realizing their ambitions at China's expense.

28

So when the haggling was all over, and everyone had gone home, the only nations in the world which had definitely committed themselves to the policy of the "Open Door" were Japan and the United States. In fact, Japan had actually gone further than we were willing to, for she had indicated her readiness to defend the "Open Door" policy by force. And, as a result of Hay's efforts, that policy had been expanded to mean not merely equal trading rights in China, but also the defense of her political independence and her geographical borders.

JAPAN AND THE "OPEN DOOR"

In lending their support to Secretary Hay and his policy of the "Open Door," the Japanese had shown themselves to be shrewd, far-seeing and perhaps a bit unscrupulous. In those days Russia was the one power which was clearly and obviously menacing China's territorial integrity, especially in Manchuria. When the Boxer Rebellion broke out, she sent large bodies of troops into Manchuria. After the rebellion was over, and the other nations had called their troops back home, the Russians in Manchuria stayed. To Japan this looked like a serious menace. Sooner or later, she saw, she would have to go to war with Russia. Meanwhile, a really hearty-sounding promise to uphold the "Open Door" would serve to avert suspicion from her own activities, and might even secure her the help of the United States when the war finally came.

THE ANGLO-JAPANESE ALLIANCE

In preparing for that war, Japan's first step was to arrange an alliance with Great Britain (1902). Known in history books as the "Anglo-Japanese Alliance," this treaty provided that in case either Great Britain or Japan should get involved in a war

1898-1904
EVE OF THE RUSSO-JAPANESE WAR

MANCHURIA

VLADIVOSTOK

MUKDEN

PORT ARTHUR

KOREA

TIBET

U. S. ANNEXES PHILIPPINES 1898
GERMANY ACQUIRES PACIFIC ISLANDS
RUSSO-JAPANESE RIVALRY   1898
    OVER KOREA (1898-1904)
TIBET BECOMES BRITISH SPHERE
    OF INFLUENCE (1904)
RUSSIAN TROOPS IN OCCUPATION OF
    MANCHURIA AND
    RAILWAY ZONES (1900-1905)

MANILA

PHILIPPINE
ISLANDS

Grant

with *one* other country over certain specific issues in the Far
East, her ally would stay neutral; but if either Great Britain
or Japan had to fight *two* countries at once in a Far Eastern
war, the other would come to the defense of her ally. Renewed and extended, the Anglo-Japanese Alliance remained
in force until 1922.

When she had concluded this alliance and finished her military preparations, Japan broke off relations with Russia, and for more than a year (1904–1905) the two countries fought it out. Japan won every major battle. She captured Port Arthur; defeated the Russian army at the famous battle of Mukden; destroyed the Russian navy. But still Russia was not beaten. And Japan was nearing the end of her resources.

Just when it seemed likely that the tide of battle would turn in favor of the Russians, President Theodore Roosevelt intervened. "Teddy" Roosevelt liked to talk about "shaking the big stick," and went out of his way to take a hand in settling international disputes. In the Far East he believed that Russia was the villain of the piece, and that if the "Japs" succeeded in checking them, the future would take care of itself. As for the "Open Door," the Japanese had not only given their word to observe it, but had been its most ardent defenders. Of course they would want some reward for their efforts—Korea, for instance. But they would grant equal trading rights in whatever territory they got. A Japanese victory would mean that the "Open Door" was safe forever.

Some such thoughts as these were probably in President Theodore Roosevelt's mind when he intervened in the Russo-Japanese War—at precisely the moment, remember, when the tide of battle seemed about to turn against Japan. Though still able to carry on the war, the Russian Czar was having trouble with revolutionaries at home, and so he accepted the President's invitation to send representatives to a peace conference to be held in the United States. The Russian general in charge of operations is said to have wept when he received the order to cease fire.

THE PORTSMOUTH CONFERENCE

The peace conference which assembled at Portsmouth, New Hampshire, in the summer of 1905, was one of the strangest episodes in our history. To a large summer hotel in a New England seaside resort came representatives and high dignitaries of two nations on the other side of the world. There for more than a month they conferred, bargained, exchanged demands and counter-demands. In the treaty which they finally produced, Russia ceded to Japan the southern half of the big island called Sakhalin (sock-ah-leen), as well as her rights and privileges in the Kwantung Peninsula—the southernmost tip of the Liaotung Peninsula. Russia also transferred to Japan the southern section of the railway she had been building to connect the Trans-Siberian Railway with Port Arthur. And she agreed not to interfere with Japan in Korea.

JAPAN BEGINS TO PUSH THE DOOR SHUT

If President Theodore Roosevelt could have foreseen what was coming next, he would probably not have been so eager to aid Japan. For what he had done was to help her assume the role previously played by Russia. From that day on, the most serious threat to the doctrine of the "Open Door" came from Japan. Her victory, which President Roosevelt had helped her clinch, made her a world power. And she lost no time in using her new-gained strength exactly as she had seen the nations of Europe doing in the previous century. Now that it was no longer useful to her, she quickly forgot her former enthusiasm for the "Open Door." From having been its warmest champion, she soon became its principal opponent. For though she continued to pay "lip service" to it, she steadily undermined it in practice.

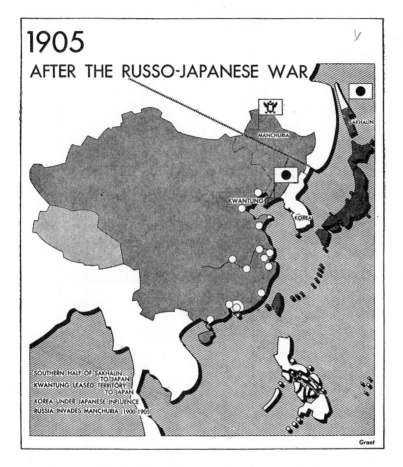

1905
AFTER THE RUSSO-JAPANESE WAR

MANCHURIA

KWANTUNG

KOREA

SAKHALIN

SOUTHERN HALF OF SAKHALIN
TO JAPAN
KWANTUNG LEASED TERRITORY
TO JAPAN
KOREA UNDER JAPANESE INFLUENCE
RUSSIA INVADES MANCHURIA (1900-1905)

Grant

First, Japan tightened her hold on southern Manchuria. She enlarged and extended the South Manchuria Railway, as she called the section she had taken from Russia. She sent in guards to police the right-of-way. Gradually she began to exercise political control, not only over the land immediately adjacent to the railroad (which a treaty she had signed

33

with China permitted her to do), but also over an ever-widening area beyond it (which no treaty gave her any sanction for). In 1909 our government tried to get other governments to join in measures which might stop this gradual extension of Japanese power in Manchuria. But the attempt failed: Japan went right on with her plans.

In 1910 she annexed Korea outright. And as there had been an "understanding" with Japan over this at the time of the Russo-Japanese War, we did not protest.

THE SCRAMBLE FOR LOANS

Meanwhile, however, the other nations had been soft-pedaling their attempts to acquire ports, "concessions" and "spheres of influence" in China and were engaged in trying to help their banker-citizens participate in the various loans which were being made to the Chinese government. In this new scramble, which lasted for a number of years, our own government was at least as active as any other. But before the race to lend money to China had gone very far, the Manchu dynasty was overthrown, and China was nominally a republic. The revolution which produced this result so altered the Far Eastern situation that we shall need a separate chapter to describe it.

IV. China Becomes a Republic

After the defeat of the Boxer Movement, which she had secretly encouraged, old Tzu Hsi decided that the only hope for China was to copy Japan and "go western." Western schools were established, western laws introduced; in fact, it was even announced that the Empress was going to give the people a share in the government—a truly revolutionary idea in an ancient autocracy like China's. But it all came too late. The Manchu government was already old and decadent at the beginning of the nineteenth century; by the beginning of the twentieth the impact of the West, its guns, its opium, its war indemnities, its trade, its missionaries—all these new and disturbing influences had just about finished the Manchu reign. Tzu Hsi died almost before her reforms were begun. She was succeeded by a four-year-old boy—as "Kang Teh" (kong-duh), he is now Japan's puppet emperor of "Manchoukuo" (mon-joe-gwoh). And the men who really ran the government after Tzu Hsi's death disapproved of her reforms and tried to slow them down. But the people had had enough of the Manchus by this time, and in 1911 they began to revolt.

CHINA'S GEORGE WASHINGTON

The two men who played the most prominent parts in the early years of the Chinese Republic were Dr. Sun Yat-sen (son-yat-sen) and General Yuan Shih-kai (you-on-shih-kye). When the revolt began, Dr. Sun was living in exile. He had been a revolutionary all his life, and some of his early activities had gotten him into trouble. But even when he was living on the other side of the world, Dr. Sun was working ceaselessly in the cause of Chinese nationalism, raising money, writing articles and in many other ways endeavoring to bring about the overthrow of the decrepit Manchu dynasty and the establishment of a genuinely democratic republic. When he heard of the revolt, he hurried back to China, where he was immediately recognized as the spiritual leader of the revolutionaries and the father of the Chinese Republic they established. People call him today the "Chinese George Washington."

35

The other man, Yuan Shih-kai, was not a revolutionary, but a conservative who had long served the Manchus. When the revolt had reached a point at which it seemed wise to the Manchus to abdicate, they put Yuan in charge of the government at Peking.

Meanwhile, Dr. Sun Yat-sen had established a new government at Nanking. There his supporters had organized themselves into a party called the "Kuomintang" (guo-min-dong) or National People's Party. This party's "platform" was the unification of all China in a single democratic republic.

Instead of fighting a civil war, Dr. Sun and General Yuan came to terms. Yuan Shih-kai was elected provisional president of the new Chinese Republic, established early in 1912. And Dr. Sun was given the job of writing China's new constitution. When Dr. Sun and his parliament tried to make General Yuan obey this constitution, they found that they were dealing with a lawless warlord. They tried to revolt against him, but Yuan had the army, and he stopped them, fast. Then, with the help of generous loans from western bankers, he made himself ruler not only of China proper, but of most that was left of the old Manchu Empire. That is why the Republic of China today still includes so much more than "China proper." In 1916, after an unsuccessful attempt to make himself Emperor, Yuan died, and for ten long years the military governors, or tuchuns (doo-juns), he had appointed to rule the various provinces of the former Manchu Empire fought among themselves.

ϰ JAPAN AND THE WORLD WAR

A year before Yuan's death, Japan took another big step toward the eventual domination of all China. At the outbreak of the World War she seized Germany's port in Shantung,

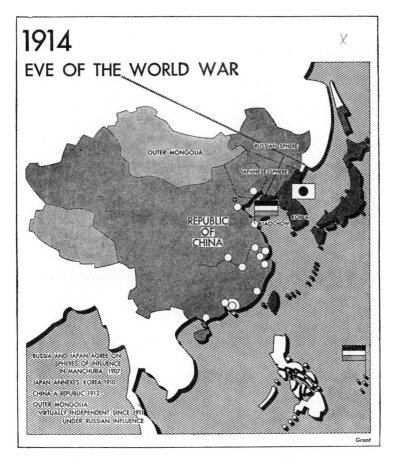

1914
EVE OF THE WORLD WAR

X

OUTER MONGOLIA

RUSSIAN SPHERE

JAPANESE SPHERE

KOREA

REPUBLIC
OF
CHINA

KIAOCHOW

RUSSIA AND JAPAN AGREE ON
SPHERES OF INFLUENCE
IN MANCHURIA 1907
JAPAN ANNEXES KOREA 1910
CHINA A REPUBLIC 1912
OUTER MONGOLIA
VIRTUALLY INDEPENDENT SINCE 1911
UNDER RUSSIAN INFLUENCE

Grant

now called Tsingtao (ching-dah-oh), Germany's economic
concessions in that province, and Germany's island possessions
in the north Pacific. Then, seeing that the nations of Europe
were involved up to their necks in the war, and couldn't possibly do more than protest, whatever she did in Asia, Japan
delivered to China her notorious "Twenty-one Demands."

37

✗ THE TWENTY-ONE DEMANDS

An American authority says that "every word of these demands was packed with anaesthesia for Chinese sovereignty." Among other things, China was to (1) let Japan do as she pleased in Shantung; (2) allow her to keep the rights and privileges she had acquired in Manchuria and also extend those rights; (3) give her mining concessions; (4) recognize her "special position" in the southern province of Fukien (foo-djen), opposite Formosa; (5) appoint Japanese advisers to the Chinese government; (6) buy 50 per cent of her munitions from Japan; and (7) allow Japan to share in the administration of the police forces of China's principal cities. If Japan had been allowed to get away with these "Twenty-one Demands," China would have ceased to be an independent nation then and there.

But she did not get away with them, not, at least, with all of them. And it was a combination of Chinese nationalism and the diplomatic intervention of the United States which stopped her. China and our own State Department both protested so vigorously that the Japanese withdrew the worst of the demands, and when they were finally presented to China in the form of an ultimatum, to be accepted in 48 hours, or else . . . , they were considerably toned down. Nevertheless they were still far-reaching enough to give Japan a strangle-hold on China which has never been completely broken since.

Having seized the German islands and leasehold, and having compelled China to grant her many special privileges, Japan took no further active part in the war. Instead she tried to weaken the Chinese government still further by helping first one warlord and then another to revolt against it.

When the World War was over and the nations which won

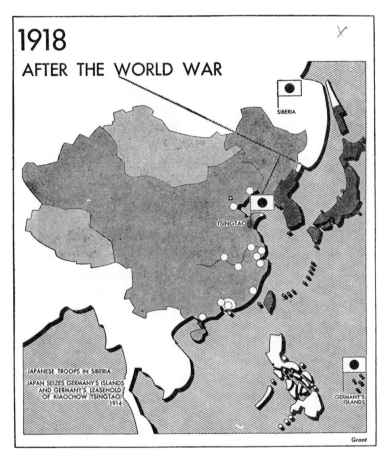

1918

AFTER THE WORLD WAR

SIBERIA

TSINGTAO

JAPANESE TROOPS IN SIBERIA

JAPAN SEIZES GERMANY'S ISLANDS
AND GERMANY'S LEASEHOLD
OF KIAOCHOW (TSINGTAO)
1914

GERMANY'S
ISLANDS

Grant

it had sent their representatives to Paris to write the terms of peace, Japan insisted on keeping the German islands and the German leasehold in Shantung she had seized. As this was directly contrary not only to the policy of the "Open Door" but also to the principle of the "self-determination of peoples," President Woodrow Wilson flatly refused to consider

39

it. But when the Japanese threatened to withdraw from the Conference if they didn't get what they wanted, Wilson backed down. This time it was China's turn to protest: in the end she refused to sign the Versailles Treaty. But Japan kept the German leasehold and privileges in Shantung until the diplomats at the Washington Conference of 1922 persuaded her to give them up. And she still has the German islands.

X THE OCCUPATION OF SIBERIA

At the time of the Paris Peace Conference she also seemed on the point of adding Siberia to her booty. When the Russian Bolsheviks seized power, in the fall of 1917, Japan proposed sending an expeditionary force into Siberia, "to restore order." Britain and France were willing, but the United States refused. The following year all four countries sent in troops, the Japanese ten times as many as any of the others. Moreover, the Japanese kept their troops there after the others had withdrawn, and for a while it looked very much as though they were planning to take over Siberia. Once again the United States protested. But Japan ignored our protests, and it was not until after the Washington Conference that her forces in eastern Siberia were finally called home.

X SUMMARY TO 1921

From the day in 1899 when Secretary Hay announced the policy of the "Open Door," to the day in the late fall of 1921 when the powers of the world met at Washington to consider ways and means to limit the naval race and divert the storm that was clearly gathering over Asia, Japan had been steadily enlarging her empire both on the continent of Asia and eastward in the Pacific. From Russia she had obtained

40

the tip of the Liaotung Peninsula, the southern half of Sakhalin Island and the southern section of the South Manchuria Railway (1905). She had annexed Korea (1910). She had seized the German leasehold and concessions in the Shantung Peninsula (1914), as well as the German islands in the Pacific (1914). With the Twenty-one Demands she had obtained extension of her rights in South Manchuria, a "free hand" in Shantung, and recognition of her "special interests" in Fukien (1915). And her troops were treading the hard soil of eastern Siberia (1918–22).

The policy of the "Open Door" may have forced Japan to go slower than she would otherwise have done, but it certainly had not prevented her from encroaching on the independence and the territory of China in the end. And it did not seem any more likely to do so in the future than it had in the past. Its only lasting effect had been to strain the relations between her government and the government of the United States, and make the Japanese people feel that the American people were going out of their way to prevent Japan from realizing her "manifest destiny."

THE EVE OF THE WASHINGTON CONFERENCE

In 1921 the relations of the two countries were so bad that there was open talk of war. Both Japan and America were rapidly building up their navies. As Great Britain was still Japan's ally, war between Japan and the United States would have compelled Great Britain to choose between fighting us and repudiating her treaty obligation to Japan. If she had chosen the former—the only honorable—course, Canada could hardly have failed to join her.

Such was the world situation when President Harding asked the great powers to meet at Washington, late in 1921.

41

V. Ten Years of Friendship

The Washington Conference, which met in the winter of
1921–22, has been called "the most important diplomatic
gathering which ever took place in the Western Hemisphere."
Looking back on it today, we can see that its achievements
were really astonishing. It was called to settle two sets of
problems, the naval race, and the threat of war in the Pacific.
And it settled them both—at least for a time.

THE WASHINGTON TREATY

Seven treaties were signed at the Washington Conference, but
only two of them are still important today. In the first of
these, the "Washington Treaty," Great Britain, the United
States, Japan, France and Italy agreed to limit their "capital
ships," or battleships and aircraft carriers, in the ratio of
5-5-3-1.7-1.7. That is, for every five tons of battleships in the
British and American navies, Japan was to have not more
than three tons and France and Italy not more than 1.7 tons
each.

Although it applied only to battleships and aircraft carriers,
and not to cruisers, destroyers, submarines and other smaller
naval vessels, the Washington Treaty stopped the worst (and
most expensive) part of the naval race for nearly fifteen
years. In 1930 a treaty signed at London extended the agreement to include the smaller ships. Both treaties expired at the
end of 1936.

THE NINE-POWER PACT

The other important treaty signed at the Washington Conference is the famous Nine-Power Pact. In it nine of the lead-
42

ing nations of the world, including Japan, solemnly agreed to maintain the "Open Door" in China, respect her "administrative and territorial integrity," and refrain from seeking special privileges from her. This was the first time the "Open Door" policy had been generally accepted by the world powers.

Besides concluding these two treaties, the Washington Conference extracted from Japan a promise to call her troops back from Siberia and return to China the German leasehold and privileges in the province of Shantung. At the same time, the Anglo-Japanese Alliance was dissolved. In return for these concessions, the powers agreed not to extend the fortifications on their islands in the Pacific Ocean, to respect one another's island possessions there, and to consult one another if those islands should be threatened.

THE "ERA OF GOOD FEELING"

For almost ten years from the time the Washington Conference adjourned, Japan stuck pretty faithfully to the promises she had made. She withdrew her troops from Siberia, returned the German Shantung leasehold to China, and did little or nothing to violate the principle of the "Open Door" or to obtain further special privileges in China. On two occasions during this decade Japanese troops did, as a matter of fact, invade Shantung, but on both occasions the militarists, temporarily in power, were defeated by the "liberals," who promptly recalled the armed forces.

In addition to keeping her promises about China in this period, Japan also joined the other nations of the world in signing the Kellogg-Briand Pact, otherwise known as the Pact of Paris. In this treaty, signed in 1928, the signatories promised never again to use war "as an instrument of national policy," and to settle all their disputes by peaceful methods. The word-

43

ing, Mr. Kellogg explained, did not deprive any nation of the right to use force in *self-defense;* and the result has been that when nations want to make war today, they omit the old-fashioned "declaration" of war, for that would be illegal. Instead, they claim that they are fighting in self-defense. But at the time it was signed the Kellogg-Briand Pact was widely hailed as a sign that the world had renounced war for good. The Pact binds the sixty-three countries which signed it "forever."

If the ten years which followed the Washington Conference were years of comparative peace and friendship between China and Japan, the relations between Japan and the United States were not so good. And the relations between the various factions in China were very bad indeed. For the friendly feeling Japan felt for us as a result of the Washington Conference was soon dispelled by our Immigration Act of 1924. And in China there was sanguinary civil war.

THE IMMIGRATION LAW

When the Central Pacific Railroad was pushing eastward from the Pacific coast, in the sixties of the last century, Chinese coolie labor was needed and welcomed, and a great many Chinese laborers came to the United States. But after the railroad was finished, and the coolies had taken other jobs, American workers began to complain of their competition. In 1882 Congress "suspended" Chinese immigration, and in 1904 it passed a law *prohibiting* the immigration of Chinese laborers forever. This the Chinese people took as an insult, and for a while they boycotted our goods. But the ban was not lifted.

Japan was eager to avoid the humiliation of having her laborers excluded as China's had been, and so she took the initiative of refusing to give them passports to go to America.

In 1907, after an outburst of anti-Japanese feeling in California, the Japanese government promised not to allow Japanese workers to emigrate to the United States. This "Gentlemen's Agreement," as it was called, reduced Japanese immigration to a trickle without offending Japanese feelings. But it left the Japanese government in a position to open the valve and pour immigrants into the United States whenever it wanted to.

To deprive the Japanese government of this power (which it gave no sign of intending to use), Congress took a step which Japan has never forgiven or forgotten: it passed a law definitely and bluntly excluding all Orientals born outside the United States from coming here to live (1924). The only exceptions were students, teachers, government officials, and the like.

This new law was clearly aimed at the Japanese. Now the Japanese would willingly have accepted a quota, and this would have achieved the same result. But outright exclusion was another matter: it stung their pride. Japan immediately protested; the protest was ignored. As an alternative to a quota system, the law has served no purpose except to give the Japanese militarists one more excuse for conquering China. They claim that since the United States has shut their people out, Japan must find room for her surplus population elsewhere. The argument is probably bogus, as the Japanese people don't seem at all eager to leave their island home, no matter how overcrowded it may be. But even bogus arguments often make good propaganda in time of war, and this one is no exception. It was handed to the Japanese militarists by our own Congress.

CHINA'S CIVIL WAR

When we last looked at China, President Yuan had just died (1916), and the military governors, or tuchuns, he had ap-

45

pointed to rule the various provinces were fighting among themselves. The prize Yuan's tuchuns were fighting for was the government he had left behind him at Peking.

During this period the Kuomintang was weak and disorganized. But in 1923 Dr. Sun obtained promises of help from the Russian Communists. With their aid he reorganized the Kuomintang, trained an army, and established a new Kuomintang government at Canton.

Dr. Sun died in 1925, but General Chiang Kai-shek (djiong-kye-sheck), who had been his protégé, succeeded him as Kuomintang leader and continued to carry out his plans. When his army was ready, Chiang began a triumphal march north (1926–27). Thanks in part to his own skill as a military leader, and thanks, also, to the inability of the tuchuns to unite in opposition to him, Chiang succeeded in winning control of most of China south of the Great Wall. By the summer of 1928 he had driven Yuan's successors out of Peking, which he renamed Peiping (bay-ping), "Northern Peace," and had established the Kuomintang government at Nanking (non-jing).

THE STRUGGLE WITH THE COMMUNISTS

On the way north, however, the Kuomintang had been very nearly wrecked by a fight-to-the-finish between the Communists and the conservatives within its own ranks. When Dr. Sun accepted Communist aid he believed that communism could never make much headway in China. But he had been wrong. Besides arms, experts and political and technical advisers (of whom the most famous was a man named Michael Borodin), Russia had also sent propaganda agents. By the spring of 1927 communism had made great progress both in and out of the Kuomintang. In March of that year some of the hot-heads in the Communist wing of the party led a brutal attack on the foreigners at Nanking. In this uprising several of the foreigners lost their lives, and many more were wounded or assaulted. Not until British and American destroyers had shelled the city did the outrages cease.

Shortly before this occurrence, Chiang Kai-shek had split with the Kuomintang radicals, with whom he had not been able to agree. Now he turned on the Communists and drove them out of the party. In this "purge" he displayed much ruthless cruelty, especially in Shanghai, where thousands of Chinese Communists were beheaded. Realizing that the game was up, Borodin escaped over the Gobi desert in a second-hand Dodge. And the Chinese Communist leaders retreated to the southern provinces, where they reorganized their forces and fought the Kuomintang government relentlessly until a truce was declared early in 1937. Besides the Communists, Chiang Kai-shek also had to contend with a number of warlords who were eager to put themselves in his place.

THE REVISION OF THE TREATIES

After establishing itself at Nanking, the Kuomintang government began to seek and obtain new treaties with the western nations, restoring to China some of the sovereign rights she had lost in the long years of the declining Manchu Empire. Thus, after nearly ninety years, she regained the right to fix her own tariffs. From Great Britain she received back Weihaiwei and four of the "concessions" secured in the days of China's weakness. In fact, she even obtained recognition of her right to abolish extraterritoriality, though no nation has so far been willing to give up its courts in China except Germany and Austria, which lost theirs in the World War, and Russia, which, under its Communist government, has divested itself of these relics of "capitalist imperialism."

Besides signing new treaties, Chiang Kai-shek also began to take steps to extend his government's authority over the three northern provinces of Manchuria. And there he bumped squarely against the imperialist designs of Japan.

SHIDEHARA AND THE "FRIENDSHIP POLICY"

During most of the period from 1921 to 1931 Japan's foreign policy was charted by a group of liberal leaders, of whom the Foreign Minister, Baron Shidehara, was the most prominent. Backed by a majority of the nation's more responsible bankers and business men, Shidehara believed that China would prove a better market for Japanese goods if Japan treated her in a friendly and conciliatory way than if she continued to carry out the aggressive policies of the Twenty-one Demands. Events seemed to prove the wisdom of his view. After the Washington Conference, and the return to China of the former German leasehold in Shantung, the Chinese dropped the boycott they had been conducting against Japanese goods. Immediately Japanese sales in China began to mount.

THE JAPANESE MILITARISTS

But not everyone in Japan agreed with Shidehara. The militarists especially were impatient with his "weakness" toward China, as well as with his efforts to reduce armaments and government expenditures on armaments. What is more important still, these men of the army and navy in Japan had never submitted to the authority of the civil government as the officers of western nations had. They were responsible only to the Emperor, and the old traditions of the ancient warrior caste made them feel actual contempt for the business men in the cabinet who were supposed to be directing the destinies of their country.

48

THE CLASH OF INTERESTS IN MANCHURIA X

Now, as we have seen, Japan had controlled the southern part of the railroad in Manchuria ever since her victory over Russia in 1905, and her "rights" in Manchuria had been confirmed in a treaty with China the same year. Since that time she had been steadily extending her influence in the area. During the long civil wars, Manchuria had been in the hands of a typical Chinese warlord, Chang Tso-lin (djong-tso-lin). Chang was jealous of the growing power of Chiang Kai-shek and was willing to oblige the Japanese if necessary to strengthen his own position. But, not being a traitor, he was not always ready to give them everything they asked for. By 1927 he had become more of a hindrance than a help to the Japanese militarists and so they engineered an explosion in which he was killed. The son who succeeded him, Chang Hsueh-liang (djong-shweh-lee-ong), was more sympathetic to the Kuomintang than his father. Ignoring warnings from Japan, Chang Hsueh-liang soon began to cooperate with the Kuomintang in its program for making Manchuria an integral part of the newly unified Chinese nation. This was too much for the Japanese militarists. For several years they tried to get their government to adopt a "positive policy"—a polite Oriental way of saying bombs and bullets. But Baron Shidehara steadfastly refused to be budged, and the militarists had to wait.

JAPAN SEES HER CHANCE X

When the great depression overwhelmed the world, in 1929 and 1930, they saw their chance. And they lost little time in taking it. More than forty years before, a far-seeing member of this same warrior class had prophesied that that chance would one day come. "Wait," he had advised the Emperor, "for the time of the confusion of Europe, which must come eventually sooner or later, and . . . we may then become the chief nation of the Orient." He could not have created a better opportunity for putting his plans into effect if he had ordered it himself. Throughout the world banks were closing their doors, factories were raking the coals out of their boilers and turning their workers on to the streets, nations were suspending payments on their debts and "going off the gold standard," tariff barriers were being run up in a desperate effort to protect the home markets, prices were falling, stocks were dropping like power-diving airplanes, and everywhere unemployment and destitution were increasing and bread-lines lengthening. "The time of the confusion of Europe" was the time of the confusion of the whole world—including Japan. For the Japanese militarists it was the big chance they had been waiting for.

As the depression dragged on, the Japanese people became more and more restless, more and more ready to believe that in a war of conquest lay the solution of all their troubles. By the fall of 1931 this idea had made such headway that the army felt powerful enough to go ahead *in spite of* Shidehara and the other "moderates" in the government. On the night of September 18, 1931, it took matters into its own hands.

The events of that fateful night started the world on a toboggan slide it hasn't hit the bottom of yet.

VI. The Manchurian Crisis X

On the night of September 18, 1931, there was an explosion on the Japanese-controlled South Manchuria Railway. To this day no one knows who was really responsible for it. But the Japanese military commander used it as an excuse to occupy all the cities in the southern part of Manchuria, and his troops moved so swiftly and so efficiently that if he didn't know the explosion was coming he must at least have laid careful plans for his military operations weeks before it occurred. In all likelihood, the explosion was part of those plans. Knowing that their forces were not strong enough to resist the powerful Japanese army, the Chinese officers in Manchuria either withdrew their troops or permitted their men to be peaceably disarmed.

CHINA APPEALS TO THE LEAGUE X

Three days after the attack began, China appealed to the League of Nations, and the League asked the United States whether we should be willing to join it in forming a commission of inquiry to investigate the circumstances of the Japanese army's action. Believing that the Japanese militarists had acted without the knowledge or consent of the civil government, and hoping that, if we were careful not to take any steps which might arouse Japan's resentment, the civil authorities of Japan would call the army back, Secretary of State Stimson refused. The League then appealed to both China and Japan to stop their hostilities and withdraw their forces, and the United States sent independent notes to the same effect. To both America and the League Japan replied that she had acted in self-defense and was already calling her army back within the railroad zone where, according to her old treaty arrangements with China, it belonged. But at the same time she refused to allow the League to investigate. China, on the other hand, claimed that she was not responsible for the outbreak, for which she blamed Japan. She explained that her troops had not resisted the Japanese army, and stated that she would welcome a League inquiry.

✗ THE LEAGUE INVOKES THE KELLOGG PACT

Instead of withdrawing, however, the Japanese forces proceeded to conquer most of Manchuria. As soon as they saw what was happening, the members of the League again appealed to the United States. This time their proposal was that we have a delegate attend the League Council when, and only when, it was considering the application of the Kellogg-Briand Pact. As we were as eager as any other signer to uphold the principles of that Pact, we promptly agreed. At the meeting the nations which had signed the Pact decided to send notes to both China and Japan calling their attention to the fact that in the Kellogg-Briand Pact they had both agreed to settle "all disputes or conflicts . . . by pacific means." Having joined in the sending of these notes, the United States returned to the sidelines to watch and wait.

⋀ JAPAN'S ARMY ADVANCES

A week later the Council of the League "directed" Japan to carry out the promised withdrawal of her troops. To this Japan replied that she would do so if China would agree to accept Japan's much expanded version of her "treaty rights" in Manchuria. But this was equivalent to using force to settle a dispute, something Japan had specifically agreed not to do

52

when she signed the Kellogg-Briand Pact. When China offered to submit the dispute over treaty rights to arbitration, a procedure which would have been legal under the Pact, Japan curtly refused. Instead, she pushed her army northward to the borders of Soviet Russia, capturing Tsitsihar (chee-chee-hah), the capital of the northernmost Manchurian province of Heilungkiang (hay-loong-djiong) and making herself boss of all but the southwest corner of the ancient home of the Manchus. While she was carrying out these military operations, her people back home were becoming more and more inflamed by the spirit of war, which took the form not merely of hostility to China but of defiance to the whole civilized world.

WE BEGIN TO ACT

Realizing at last that Japan's action in Manchuria was rapidly destroying the peace-preserving machinery which the nations had painstakingly erected in the years after the World War, Secretary Stimson then took two steps which he hoped would stem the tide before it was too late. He called in the Japanese Ambassador and told him that his country was breaking her sacred word. And he authorized our Ambassador to London, Mr. Charles G. Dawes, to cooperate with the League.

Unfortunately, neither step had any lasting effect. If the civil government of Japan tried to control the Japanese army, it failed. And Mr. Dawes had no sooner received his authority to sit in on the meetings of the League than he ran up against the blank wall of economic sanctions.

Economic sanctions were one of several methods the League's Covenant provided for stopping an aggressor. What they amounted to was a boycott by the League members of part or all of their trade with the offending nation. But in the case of

Japan sanctions could not succeed without the cooperation of the United States, for Japan at that time did roughly a third of her foreign trade with us: if other countries had cut off their business with Japan, that business would simply have been transferred to the United States. And our government had no authority to stop or control it, nor any reason to hope that it could obtain the authority. Congress was not in session, and even if it had been there was very little reason to believe that it would authorize the State Department to cooperate with the League to that extent.

So when Mr. Dawes was asked whether the United States would join the League in imposing sanctions on Japan, and he had referred the question to the State Department, Secretary Stimson had to say no.

For a few brief days after the sanctions proposal had been discarded, Japan's actions gave hope that the "collective system" might still be saved. For, late in November, the Japanese representatives at Geneva suddenly shifted their ground and announced that they would accept a League investigation after all. Two and a half weeks later they joined the other members of the League Council in appointing a commission of inquiry. Headed by an Englishman, Lord Lytton, the commission consisted of representatives of Great Britain, Germany, France, Italy and the United States. The commissioners left at once for the Far East, where they received the assistance of both China and Japan in making their investigation.

Besides reversing themselves on the question of a League of Nations inquiry, the Japanese civil authorities also stopped the invasion of Manchuria. After the conquest of Heilungkiang, another branch of the Japanese army had started out toward Chinchow (gin-joe), a city in the southwestern part of Manchuria, the only section of the country which had not yet been

54

occupied by Japanese troops. On November 27, 1931 this army was recalled, and for two weeks the world believed that the fighting in the East was over.

JAPAN TAKES THE PLUNGE

But it was only a flash in the pan, the swan-song of the Japanese advocates of a "friendship policy" toward China. For the war spirit had reached such a fever-heat in Japan that the Cabinet in which Baron Shidehara was Foreign Minister was soon overthrown, to be succeeded by a group of men who were much more friendly to the "positive policy" of the army. This new government let the army off the leash, and within three weeks the whole of Manchuria was occupied by Japanese troops. Since that time, Japan's militarists have steadily increased their influence over Japan's government. In 1936 some of the younger and more rabid of them actually resorted to assassination and mutiny to increase their influence still further.

"NON-RECOGNITION"

America's reaction to Japan's conquest of Manchuria was the famous "Stimson doctrine" of "non-recognition." On January 7, 1932, Secretary Stimson notified both China and Japan that if the Japanese violated the Kellogg-Briand Pact, infringed on the territorial or administrative integrity of China, or closed the "Open Door," the United States would never accept the new situation. Instead, we would refuse to admit that Japan had any rights, or any lands, she hadn't had before.

Secretary Stimson seems to have hoped that this pronouncement would check Japan; but, if it had any effect at all, it only encouraged her to fresh aggression. For it showed the world that, far from cooperating to stop her, the two great English-speaking nations, Great Britain and the United States, were going their separate ways, agreeing only in their determination to avoid decisive—and hence dangerous—action. And the Japanese knew that the only thing they really had to fear was close, and active, cooperation between the British Empire and the United States: that alone could stop them.

What actually happened was this: instead of coming out with a letter of its own, backing him up to the hilt, as Mr. Stimson hoped and expected it would, the British Foreign Office issued a freezing statement in which it explained that, as Japan had promised not to violate the "Open Door," it saw no reason for addressing a note to Tokyo at all!

And, of course, the Japanese were quick to take advantage of the rift: they sent Mr. Stimson a reply which "came within an ace of insolence." In that reply they adopted a new line of argument, but one they have made the most of since. China, they said, was so "unsettled and distracted" that it was not an organized state, and therefore the League Covenant, the Nine-Power Treaty, and the Kellogg-Briand Pact did not apply. The fact that China had been even more disorganized at the time Japan entered into these agreements the Japanese Foreign Office studiously ignored.

JAPAN ATTACKS SHANGHAI

A few days after delivering this slap, Japan attacked the great modern port of Shanghai. Patriotic Chinese citizens there had started a boycott of Japanese goods as soon as the occupation of Manchuria began. Apparently hoping to force them to drop the boycott and thus bring glory on the navy, which was jealous of the army's successes in Manchuria, the Japanese naval commander delivered an ultimatum to the mayor of

Shanghai. When, to his evident disappointment, the ultimatum was accepted, the Japanese commander went right ahead and tried to seize Chapei (chah-bay), a thickly settled Chinese section of the city. For over a month the Japanese at Shanghai were stopped by China's Nineteenth Route Army. Alarmed, they bombed the Chinese town, killing thousands of helpless and defenseless civilians and arousing the horror of the world. But not until they had sent heavy reinforcements to outflank them were they able to make the Chinese defenders retreat. As soon as they had "saved face" in this way they stopped firing. By the end of May, 1932, the last of the troops they had sent to the Shanghai campaign had gone home.

JAPAN CREATES "MANCHOUKUO" X

Though she failed to take Shanghai in 1932, Japan made good use of that year elsewhere: she consolidated her victory in Manchuria. In mid-February she announced the creation of the puppet state of "Manchoukuo" (mon-joe-gwoh). In March she set up "Mr. Henry Pu-yi" (poo-ye), the last of the Manchu emperors of China, as regent of the new state. (Later she made him "Emperor" under the name of "Kang Teh.") In June she had "Manchoukuo" seize the customs and salt tax revenues of Manchuria, which had previously gone to the Chinese government. And in August she went through the motions of "recognizing" "Manchoukuo" and concluding a treaty with it.

As they had failed to stop the conquest, there was little left for either the United States or the League to do but complete the record. For this, Mr. Stimson chose the device of writing an open letter to Senator Borah, the chairman of the Senate Foreign Relations Committee, repeating the non-recognition policy which had brought a cold-shoulder from Great Britain and rude noises from Japan, and stating that the United States would continue to adhere to it. As for the League, it kept its own record straight by adopting Mr. Stimson's non-recognition doctrine and accepting the Lytton Report.

THE LYTTON REPORT

Submitted to the League of Nations early in October, 1932, the Lytton Commission's report (1) dismissed the claim that China was not an organized state; (2) found her entitled to sovereignty over Manchuria; (3) declared that Japan's action there was not legitimate self-defense; (4) stated that "Manchoukuo" was a puppet of Japan; and (5) concluded that "a large area of what was indisputably Chinese territory has been forcibly seized and occupied by the armed forces of Japan and has, in consequence of this operation, been separated from and declared independent of the rest of China." In order to right the wrongs which had been done, and yet avoid returning to the very conditions which had produced the conflict, the Commission recommended that Japan call her troops back to the railroad zone, and that China resume her sovereignty over Manchuria—granting it sufficient "autonomy," however, to protect the rights and interests of Japan and other nations there.

JAPAN RESIGNS FROM THE LEAGUE

In a final effort to save its damaged reputation, the League postponed action on the Lytton Commission's report while a special committee appointed for the purpose tried to persuade Japan to accept conciliation. Instead of doing so, however, Japan proceeded to attack China again. In February, 1933, she

58

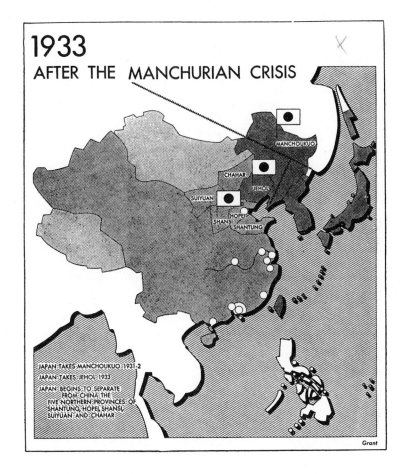

1933
AFTER THE MANCHURIAN CRISIS

MANCHOUKUO

CHAHAR

JEHOL

SUIYUAN

HOPEI
SHANSI
SHANTUNG

JAPAN TAKES MANCHOUKUO 1931-2
JAPAN TAKES JEHOL 1933
JAPAN BEGINS TO SEPARATE
FROM CHINA THE
FIVE NORTHERN PROVINCES OF
SHANTUNG, HOPEI, SHANSI,
SUIYUAN AND CHAHAR

Grant

captured the North China province of Jehol (reh-huh), adding
it to her puppet state of "Manchoukuo." Toward the end of
that same month the League finally abandoned the hope of
"conciliating" Japan and adopted the Lytton Commission's
report, over Japan's strenuous objections. Simultaneously,
Secretary Stimson issued a statement in which he said that the

59

United States was "in general accord" with the conclusions of the report and the recommendation it contained for settling the dispute. A month later (March 27, 1933), Japan notified the League that she was going to resign. By League rules the resignation took effect two years later.

Thus Japan had successfully defied the world. Ignoring her treaty obligations and the protests of the League of Nations and our own Department of State, she had conquered from China a piece of territory larger than France and Germany combined. And she had made it perfectly clear that nothing could stop her now but force or—possibly—sanctions. "Sticks and stones can break my bones," she had tauntingly chanted, "but words can never hurt me." And sticks and stones the world had failed to throw. Preoccupation with troubles nearer home, timidity, hesitation and mutual distrust—these are some of the factors which contributed to the failure.

VII. War in China

After Japan had added Jehol to her new continental empire, thus bringing it south to the Great Wall, she marched her army to the gates of Peiping in China proper. On May 31, 1933, she forced the Chinese government to sign a truce in which it agreed to withdraw its armed forces from the vicinity of the Great Wall and establish a "demilitarized zone" south of that ancient barrier. Having gained this additional victory, Japan began applying to the five North China provinces of Shantung (shahn-doong), Hopei (huh-bay), Shansi (shahn-she), Suiyuan (swee-oo-ahn), and Chahar (chah-hah) the "formula" for imperial expansion she had used with

Korea: she attempted to get those provinces to declare themselves "autonomous" and become her puppets.

CHINA PREPARES TO RESIST JAPAN

Meanwhile, however, China was preparing for a new test of strength with Japan. Under the leadership of Chiang Kai-shek and his Wellesley-graduate wife, the ancient Chinese virtues were revived in a new form, called the "New Life" movement. With the assistance of a group of German officers, a part of the Chinese army was modernized and a brand new air force acquired, chiefly from Italy and the United States. With the help of the League, China started to build new roads, improve her waterways, and take measures to prevent the terrible floods which have done so much damage to Chinese property and taken such a high toll of Chinese life in the past. A beginning was even made with a program to improve the lot of the Chinese peasants by teaching them better methods of farming. In many ways, China was at last doing what Japan had done fifty years before: go modern, go western, grow strong.

JAPAN TRIES TO HINDER CHINA

This burst of activity in China alarmed Japan, for had it succeeded it would have prevented her from achieving her imperial ambitions at China's expense. And so she did her best to hold it back. Growing opium in Manchuria, Japanese merchants sold it in its most virulent forms of morphine and heroin to the Chinese people of the demilitarized zone south of the Great Wall, and through them to many other Chinese farther from her area of control. Japan also encouraged and abetted smuggling on a vast scale, apparently in the hope of cutting down the Chinese government's revenue and undermining its authority. She protested loud and long against the "technical" assistance the League was lending China—despite the fact that that assistance concerned only such seemingly innocent subjects as roads, waterways, education, rural credit, hygiene and flood control.

When Japan's efforts to detach the five provinces of North China by intrigue had failed, and her protests against China's development had fallen on deaf ears, her militarists again resorted to bullets and bombs.

The summer of 1937 was at least as favorable a time for them to act as the fall of 1931 had been. For Europe was in an even worse mess than before. And the United States had taken several steps any one of which might have seemed like a sign that, whatever Japan might do, we would not again try to stop her. We had apparently adopted a still more cautious policy toward events in the Far East; we had decided to get out of the Philippines; and by the passage of our Neutrality Act we had declared to all the world that in future wars we would be scrupulously neutral.

THE "JAPANESE MONROE DOCTRINE"

The first test of our new Far Eastern policy came early in 1934, when Japan announced that in future she and she alone would be the "guardian of the peace of the Pacific." This "hands off" policy she called the "Japanese Monroe Doctrine." But the difference was more important than the similarity. For our own Monroe Doctrine was not intended to help us conquer South America; Japan's, on the other hand, was equivalent to notice that she was out to dominate China and would not accept interference in her plans from anybody.

62

SECRETARY HULL PLAYS SAFE

It was also in violation of the "Open Door." If Mr. Stimson had still been our Secretary of State when it was announced, it would probably have brought a vigorous letter from him. But Mr. Stimson was not our Secretary of State, and the new Administration which had come into office with President Franklin D. Roosevelt in the spring of 1933 took a somewhat different attitude toward events in the Far East. Seeing that the Stimson policy of moral pressure had failed, and realizing that the country would not be willing to back up words with deeds, Secretary Cordell Hull, the new head of the State Department, began his term of office by handling Japan with gloves. When the "Japanese Monroe Doctrine" was announced, in April, 1934, he sent as mild a note as could be devised in the circumstances. And a year and a half later, when Japan's activities in North China could no longer be ignored, he wrote again, but in terms even more gentle than those he had used before. Thus he kept the record straight without running the risk of having to swallow his words in case Japan should choose not to heed them.

WE FREE THE PHILIPPINES

The second step back from the Orient was the Philippine Independence Act. Passed March 24, 1934, this Act established procedure which will make the islands entirely independent by 1946. The only right reserved is the right to retain naval bases there if we wish. In spite of this provision, however, the step could not fail to seem like the beginning of a retreat from the Orient, and it probably helped to reduce still further our influence with Japan, already small after the failure of our diplomacy in the Manchurian crisis.

63

WE ADOPT NEUTRALITY

The third step, the passage of the Neutrality Act, seemed to confirm the impression made by the others that in any future war against China, Japan would not have to worry very much about the United States. In the summer of 1935 there was a great wave of anti-war feeling in America. This feeling was inspired partly by the Senate's investigation of the munitions business, and partly by a growing fear that another war was just around the corner. And it soon made itself felt in Congress, in spite of behind-the-scenes opposition from the President and the State Department. The result was the Neutrality Act.

Adopted hastily as a Congressional resolution in August, 1935, when Italy was openly preparing to conquer Ethiopia, the Neutrality Act was passed in "permanent" form on May 1, 1937. It was intended to keep us out of war by prohibiting Americans from selling munitions to warring nations, lending them money, or carrying their supplies in American ships. To Japan this legislation seemed to mean that if she should again attack China, the United States would not interfere.

If the situation was ripe for another Japanese advance in the summer of 1937, there were also two urgent reasons why Japan should try to make it: the United States navy was growing stronger; and, in North China, the Kuomintang's influence was spreading.

WE BUILD UP OUR NAVY

As we have seen, the Washington Treaty of 1922 limited "capital ships" to the 5-5-3 ratio, and the London Treaty of 1930 extended the limitation to ships of smaller size. Now Japan had built right up to the limits in all categories, while
64

the United States had lagged behind. The result was that, when Franklin D. Roosevelt became President, the Japanese navy was nearer three-fourths than three-fifths of ours. To change this situation, and perhaps also to prepare for the day when Japan would again be fighting in China, President Roosevelt persuaded Congress to pass the largest peace-time naval appropriations in our history. Since 1934 the United States navy has been growing fast.

JAPAN BUILDS, TOO

So, for that matter, has Japan's. The naval treaties of 1922 and 1930 were due to expire on the last day of December, 1936, and a year before that time the nations which had signed them met in London again to consider what should be done. At the conference, Japan demanded the right to have a navy as large as Britain's or America's. When her demand was refused she walked out. As a result, the treaties were not renewed. But though Japan began to build as fast as she could, she could not hope to beat the United States at that game. The longer she waited, the weaker she would be, relatively. And the knowledge that this was so may have been one of the reasons why her militarists struck when they did.

The other reason was the Kuomintang threat to her influence in North China.

Ever since the truce of May 31, 1933, Chiang Kai-shek had not only been fighting the Chinese Communists, but also suppressing the many anti-Japanese societies which had sprung up during the Manchurian war. This was gravy to the Japanese, but gall to the Chinese Nationalists, who wanted their country to resist Japan. In December, 1936, our old friend, Chang Hsueh-liang, the former military governor of Man-

65

churia, actually kidnapped General Chiang at Sian (she-ahn), and held him captive until, apparently, he had promised to reverse his policy, cooperate with the Communists, and resist the Japanese. At any rate, as soon as he was released, General Chiang began to negotiate with the Chinese Communists with a view to united resistance against Japan. And he also took a much firmer attitude toward Japanese attempts to separate the provinces of North China from the government at Nanking.

THE ANTI-COMMUNISM AGREEMENT

Faced with these new threats to their ambitions, Japan's militarists and their supporters apparently decided to "teach China a lesson." Their government had already signed an agreement with Germany in which the two countries agreed to "cooperate against communism." On the surface this agreement seemed innocent enough; but many European statesmen interpreted it as a defensive alliance against Soviet Russia. Secret clauses, they suspected, provided that if Japan should attack China and Russia should come to China's defense, Germany would attack Russia in the West.

THE LUKOUCHIAO INCIDENT

With this assurance against Russian intervention, the Japanese war-mongers made use of an "incident" in North China to press new and far-reaching demands on the Nanking government. On the 7th of July, 1937, Japanese troops engaging in night manoeuvres near Lukouchiao (loo-go-cha-oh), in Hopei province (where they had no treaty right to be), clashed with a part of the Chinese Twenty-ninth Army. After a series of obscure negotiations and a number of new clashes, Japan issued an ultimatum. In it she demanded: (1) the withdrawal
66

of the Chinese army in Hopei; (2) punishment of the Chinese responsible for the conflict; (3) "adequate" control of all anti-Japanese activities in North China; (4) enforcement of measures against communism. When General Chiang accepted these terms, the Japanese issued a second ultimatum in which they demanded complete withdrawal of all Chinese troops from the Peiping area within forty-eight hours. This second ultimatum put Chiang on the spot. China was not yet ready to defy Japan; but, as the kidnapping episode had shown, the Chinese people would not stand for much more kowtowing to her, either.

As a matter of fact, Chiang didn't have to decide just then. Even before this second ultimatum expired, the Japanese attacked the Chinese forces near Peiping. Unable to resist them effectively, the Chinese troops withdrew from the city, and by the end of the month Japan was in undisputed control of most of the Peiping area.

THE SECOND BATTLE OF SHANGHAI

From Peiping the Japanese army advanced south and west, conquering not only Hopei and Chahar but also Suiyuan and part of Shansi. In Suiyuan and Chahar, two provinces of Inner Mongolia, Japan set up a puppet state under a Mongol prince called Teh Wang (duh-wong). Tsinan (gee-non), the capital of the fifth and last North China province of Shantung, fell just before the end of the year. Reports also indicated that Japanese troops were entering Ningshia (ning-she-ah), the westernmost province of Inner Mongolia, thus driving a wedge between China and Soviet Russia.

Meanwhile, however, fierce and bitter fighting had again broken out at Shanghai. It began with an "incident" on August 10, when two members of the Japanese navy were killed by

Chinese soldiers. Again Japan issued an ultimatum. At the same time she increased her naval squadron in the Shanghai harbor and landed marines, ammunition and supplies. When Chinese troops began entering the Shanghai area, Japan invaded the Chinese section of Chapei. The battle which followed was as bloody as any that has occurred in the long history of war. Airplane bombs were freely used by both sides. On a single day more than six hundred civilians were slaughtered when Chinese planes carrying bombs intended for Japanese warships in the harbor accidentally dropped their loads in the crowded International Settlement. Among the dead were three Americans. A few days later a shell hit the U. S. warship *Augusta*, killing an American sailor. Three days later still, another bomb was dropped in the International Settlement, killing two hundred civilians and wounding nearly five hundred. On still another occasion, Japanese planes apparently deliberately bombed a group of Chinese civilian refugees gathered at a Shanghai railway station. Over three hundred people were killed, and the tracks and platforms were littered with bits of their bodies. The bombing was repeated at another railway station a few days later, when three hundred more Chinese civilians were slaughtered, and some four hundred wounded.

SECRETARY HULL'S CIRCULAR LETTERS

In invading North China, and later Shanghai, Japan had challenged again both the League of Nations and the signers of the Nine-Power Pact. Her new challenge did not go unanswered, but the answer was even more cautious than it had been in 1931–32. Shortly after the "incident" at Lukouchiao, Secretary Hull sent a statement to all the nations of the world in which, without mentioning China or Japan by name, he listed a number of principles which he said should govern international conduct. One of these principles was the sanctity of treaties. Sixty-two nations replied, endorsing Mr. Hull's principles, but, though she too accepted them, Japan insisted that "the actual particular circumstances of the region" must always be taken into consideration.

When the battle of Shanghai was at its height, Mr. Hull wrote again. This time, while still being careful not to offend anyone, he went a little further. The United States, he said, believed that the principles set forth in his previous letter applied to the Far East as much as anywhere else.

Thus, in careful diplomatic language, Mr. Hull let Japan know that, in spite of our Neutrality Act, we still felt a moral responsibility for maintaining the "administrative and territorial integrity" of China and the principle of the "Open Door." He also hinted pretty clearly that, in our opinion, Japan was again breaking a good many treaties.

JAPAN TWISTS THE LION'S TAIL

Three days after Mr. Hull's second note, a Japanese aviator machine-gunned the British Ambassador to China as he was driving in his official car outside the area of hostilities. At this amazing affront to the proud British Empire, the world held its breath. It seemed incredible that such an act of defiance could pass without the most serious consequences. The British government dispatched an indignant note, charging Japan with flagrant disregard of "one of the oldest and best established rules of international law," that attacks on noncombatants "are absolutely prohibited," and demanding a "formal apology," suitable punishment for those responsible, and an assurance that a similar attack would not be made in the future.

69

All Britain got for her pains was a grudging reply. Instead of the "formal apology," Japan expressed mild regret that the attack had occurred; and instead of the punishment and the assurance demanded, she said that her investigation had failed to prove that the attack was made by a Japanese airman. The tone of her note was one of defiance. And, without a murmur, Great Britain accepted it. From that moment Japan had every reason to believe that she could afford to do as she liked in China.

JAPAN ENLARGES HER OBJECTIVES

While this exchange was going on, Japan announced that she would blockade the Chinese coast. She soon made good her threat by establishing an actual blockade from Manchoukuo in the north to French Indo-China in the south. Though the blockade was supposed to apply only to Chinese ships, it seemed likely to lead to more international complications sooner or later. On September 5 Japan's Foreign Minister announced that his country's object was to break Chinese resistance once and for all. Later, Japanese spokesmen explained that this meant replacing the Kuomintang government with one more friendly to Japan. What it actually meant was, apparently, that this time Japan was going to make all China a "protectorate" of her own.

CHINA AGAIN APPEALS TO THE LEAGUE

A week after this announcement, China once again appealed to the League. For the moment, the best she could expect was the re-convening of the Far Eastern Advisory Committee which had been set up at the time the League adopted the Lytton Report. As there had been an American on the committee at

70

the time, the League asked us if we would continue to serve on it, and we replied that we would resume limited cooperation such as we had carried on before.

NEUTRALITY OR COOPERATION?

During the difficult days of the fighting in Shanghai, we had been trying to maintain a middle course, keeping the record straight by mildly worded and indirect protests, but at the same time doing everything we could to get Americans out of the danger zone and avoid the possibility of an "incident." President Roosevelt had not invoked the Neutrality Act. On the other hand, he had forbidden American government-owned ships to carry munitions to either China or Japan, and he had warned other American ships that if they carried munitions to the belligerents the government could not be responsible for their safety.

If this was not neutrality, at least it was moderate isolationism. But now the League had asked us to take a hand in judging the merits of the China-Japan fight, and we had agreed to do so. This was international cooperation, the opposite of isolation. Our policy in the Far East was getting more and more confused. What *was* our policy, anyway, neutrality or intervention? Or neither?

THE PRESIDENT'S ANSWER

One answer—the President's—came on October 5. Speaking in Chicago on that day, President Roosevelt completely repudiated the whole philosophy on which neutrality was based. "The present reign of terror and lawlessness" threatens "the very foundations of civilization," he said, and may plunge the world into chaos. If this happens, "let no one imagine that

71

America will escape. . . . The epidemic of world lawlessness is spreading. . . . When an epidemic of physical disease starts to spread, the community joins in a quarantine of the patients. . . . If civilization is to survive . . . there must be positive endeavors to preserve peace. America hates war. America hopes for peace. Therefore, America actively engages in the search for peace."

Though there was a good deal of doubt about the exact meaning of the President's reference to a "quarantine," his general meaning seemed perfectly clear: despite Congress and the Neutrality Act, we could not be neutral in the Far East. Instead of trying to be, we were going to take the lead in stopping Japan from conquering China.

THE LEAGUE ACTS

On the same day the President made his speech, the League's Far Eastern Advisory Committee submitted its report. It declared that in invading China Japan had violated her treaty obligations, urged League members not to take "any action which might have the effect of weakening China's resistance," and asked them to "consider how far they can individually extend aid to China." It also suggested that the nations which had signed the Nine-Power Pact, and any other nations which have special interests in the Far East (such as Russia), should meet to consider the situation Japan's action had created.

Doubtless encouraged by President Roosevelt's attitude, the League adopted this report the next day, and, in doing so, it asked the Nine-Power Treaty signers, including the United States, to call the suggested meeting. Almost simultaneously our State Department issued a statement frankly accusing Japan of breaking the Nine-Power Treaty and the Kellogg Pact. Some days later the Department accepted the invitation to the Nine-

72

Power Conference, which was scheduled to meet at Brussels.

But, good politician though he is, this time President Roosevelt had slipped: in rejecting isolationism and declaring for international cooperation, he had apparently misjudged the country's attitude toward the war in China. Almost as soon as his Chicago speech was off the presses, evidences of widespread distrust of international action began coming to him. Private individuals wrote letters; peace societies expressed alarm; Senators and Congressmen called at the White House. For a while the President stuck to his guns. But by the time the Nine-Power Conference had assembled, both the President and the State Department had realized that they had overreached themselves. Of course, it was too late then to back out. The only thing left to do was to instruct our delegates not to commit us to any kind of action, even if that meant letting the conference flop.

THE BRUSSELS CONFERENCE

And flop it did. By the time the conference met, Japan had already driven the Chinese out of Shanghai and was pursuing them up the Yangtze River as they fled westward toward Nanking. As for China, her government had announced that it was moving its various ministries from Nanking to three separate cities in the interior, to avoid the danger of capture or bombing. After urging Japan to attend, and being refused, the conference adopted a tame declaration to the effect that Japan was "out of step with the rest of the world" and listing reasons why she should consent to discuss her actions in China. Once again Japan refused to do so. Thus apparently condemned to futility, the Brussels conference adopted a noble-sounding report unholding the principles of the Nine-

Power Treaty and condemning the use of force. Having done this, it adjourned.

And Japan, undaunted, continued her aggression.

⅄ THE FALL OF NANKING

Two weeks later, amid scenes of indescribable horror, Nanking fell. Shortly before, Japan had established at Peiping (which she renamed Peking) a puppet government made up of anti-Kuomintang Chinese but clearly dominated and directed by the Japanese army. After the fall of Nanking, she established still another puppet government there. One or the other of these provisional governments seemed likely to claim authority over more and more of China as the Japanese forces extended their conquest.

⅄ THE "PANAY" INCIDENT

Meanwhile, however, airmen of the Japanese navy had precipitated an international crisis of the utmost gravity. While their army was storming the battered walls of Nanking, Japanese planes bombed and sank the *Panay* (pun-eye), a United States gunboat built for service on the Yangtze River, and attacked and destroyed three Standard Oil boats which were standing near by. Three Americans lost their lives as a result of the attack. Of the survivors, both crew and passengers, more than half were wounded, some seriously. The same day several British naval vessels and merchant ships were machine-gunned farther up the river.

When first reports of this incident reached Washington, it was assumed that the bombing had been an accident. Acting on instructions from the President, the State Department sent Japan a stern note in which it demanded a full apology, pun-

74

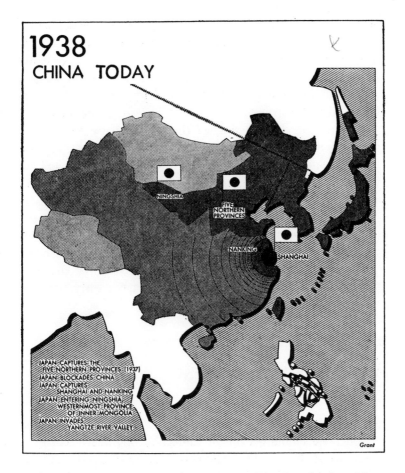

1938
CHINA TODAY

NINGSHIA

FIVE
NORTHERN
PROVINCES

NANKING

SHANGHAI

JAPAN CAPTURES THE
FIVE NORTHERN PROVINCES (1937)
JAPAN BLOCKADES CHINA
JAPAN CAPTURES
SHANGHAI AND NANKING
JAPAN ENTERING NINGSHIA,
WESTERNMOST PROVINCE
OF INNER MONGOLIA
JAPAN INVADES
YANGTZE RIVER VALLEY

Grant

ishment of the men who were responsible for the bombing, an indemnity, and a guarantee that steps would be taken to prevent similar occurrences in the future. Evidently alarmed at the possible consequences of the bombing, the Japanese Foreign Office apologized even before our note was delivered.

Later in the week the *Panay* incident assumed a more

75

ominous aspect when official reports established that the bombing was not an accident, but a deliberate attack. According to these reports, the Japanese planes flew so low that they could not have failed to see the huge American flags on the *Panay's* awnings before they released their bombs. Press accounts also indicated that Japanese surface craft joined in the attack.

All this not only heightened the tension between the two governments but produced daily streamer headlines in hundreds of American newspapers. Two weeks after the attack occurred Japan formally accepted all of the American demands, and the State Department announced that the incident was "closed." What the ultimate effect of it would be on American-Japanese relations it was, of course, too early to say. But one thing it had done: it had demonstrated with startling clarity how easily we may again be started down the path which leads to war, much as we were in the early years of the World War.

VIII. Which Way America?

Such incidents as the sinking of the *Panay* raise the question whether we should get out of China. As long as we remain in China we shall be running the risk of being dragged into war. Then why don't we clear out? Why is it that our President and our State Department are willing to have the Neutrality Act invoked when the fighting is in Ethiopia, or Spain, but not when it is in China? What is the reason for taking one attitude toward the war danger in Europe, or Africa, and quite a different attitude toward the war danger in Asia?

VALUE OF U. S. FOREIGN TRADE
(AVERAGE 1931-35)

EXPORTS TO

UNITED KINGDOM $374,400,000

CANADA $294,800,000

JAPAN $169,600,000

GERMANY $128,100,000

FRANCE $117,600,000

CHINA $75,600,000

IMPORTS FROM

CANADA $228,800,000

JAPAN $148,200,000

UNITED KINGDOM $118,400,000

GERMANY $85,100,000

FRANCE $58,600,000

CHINA $55,500,000

Each symbol represents
50 million dollars worth of goods

Grant

TO PROTECT OUR TRADE?

Is it because we do so much more business with China than we do with Europe?

No. We don't. Forty years ago it *was* trade, or rather the hope of trade, which made us take the lead in defending China's integrity. In those days people thought they saw in China a vast potential market and an inexhaustible source of raw materials. But their hopes were sadly disappointed. Only peaceful and prosperous nations make good customers, and China has been in one kind of turmoil or another almost since the beginning of our relations with her.

Look at the chart on page 77: you will see that our trade with China is at the bottom of the list. The fact is, our trade with Japan is twice as large as our trade with China. If it were only trade we're thinking of, we'd be chumps to risk the good will of Japan to save our trade with China.

TO PROTECT OUR INVESTMENTS?

If it isn't our trade with China that makes us take a special interest in her case, maybe it's our investments in China. After all, haven't we got an awful lot of money tied up there?

Wrong again. As the second chart shows, our investments in China are just a drop in the bucket compared with our investments elsewhere. Even in Japan our investments are more than twice as great. Once again, we've got more to lose than to gain by a quarrel with Japan over China.

But if it isn't trade, or the hope of trade, and it isn't investments, what is it? There must be *some* reason why we get so much more excited about China than we do about other countries.

There is.

U. S. FOREIGN INVESTMENTS 1933

Each certificate represents 250 million dollars in U.S. private long term investments

CANADA AND NEWFOUNDLAND $3,950,000,000

GERMANY $1,241,000,000

GREAT BRITAIN $612,000,000

JAPAN $418,000,000

FRANCE $348,000,000

BELGIUM $220,000,000

DENMARK $148,000,000

CHINA $132,000,000

Grant

First of all, there's habit, tradition. We've been champion-
ing China so long that it's pretty hard to stop. This is partic-
ularly true of our State Department. Tradition looms large in
the calculations of diplomats, and it's often even harder for
them to break with it than it is for lesser men.

TO MAINTAIN OUR PRESTIGE

In the case of China, too, a break from our traditional policy
would also mean a loss of prestige. And that is the second reason why the State Department doesn't want to do it. We've
talked so long about China, protested so many times against
every threat to her "integrity," that we really can't abandon
her altogether without losing at least a part of the world's good
opinion of us.

In fact, if we were going to change our policy and clear
out, we ought to have done it when the shooting first began.
Every day that has passed since has made it harder. After the
Panay incident, to invoke the Neutrality Act and turn our
backs on Asia would look very much like retreating under
fire. It would look as though the United States were afraid of
Japan. And no nation, even a small and weak one, wants to
appear in that light.

IF WE DON'T, WHO WILL?

But, aside from the heavy hand of tradition, and the question
of national prestige, there is a third reason why the State
Department and the President have failed to apply the Neutrality Act to the fighting in Eastern Asia. When there is
trouble in Europe, we have, naturally, left it to England
and France to take the lead in trying to preserve peace. But

in Asia they can't—they're too much absorbed in the troubles nearer home. We, on the other hand, are free to act. If we don't take the lead in stopping Japan, who will? And if nobody does, what will happen next? Won't the last hope of getting the world to live in peace go up in smoke? Won't we find that, by our inaction, we have let the world sink back into complete lawlessness, the rule of force?

NOW OR LATER?

If you could sit down with some high official in the State Department and have a frank talk, this is the aspect of the Far Eastern riddle he would almost certainly stress. If you could then go across the street to the White House and talk to the President, he might add something else. He might say that if we don't stop Japan's progress now, when we still have a chance to get help from Great Britain and possibly also France, we may find that we shall have to deal with her single-handed later.

What would he mean?

Just this. You know that for many years influential Japanese have been urging their country to prepare to rule the world: two such statements have been quoted in this book, but many more could easily be found. You also know that the Japanese government has little or no control over the army and navy.

Now consider this. Japan has some sort of agreement with both Italy and Germany; on the surface it is nothing more than an agreement to combat communism. What the real meaning of it is we don't know. But we do know that all three countries are out to get what they can, by threats if possible, by force if necessary. And it seems likely that they will cooperate very closely. If they do, they may be able to frighten

England, France and Russia into immobility. In fact, they've already done it.

Now all three of these "fascist" states have their eyes on South America. They hope to find markets there which have been denied them elsewhere. In Brazil, German economic penetration has already begun. And in Brazil and certain other South American countries Germany, Italy and Japan have many sympathizers. Suppose that the German, Italian and Japanese economic penetration into South America succeeds. Then suppose that one of the pro-fascist dictators down there is faced with revolution. If he should be overthrown, the German, Italian and Japanese interests in his country might suffer. Would Germany, Italy or Japan send battleships and marines to help him keep his power? And, if they did, what about the Monroe Doctrine? Wouldn't we be obliged to fight?

This is an argument which not everyone who thinks we should do something about Japan takes much stock in. But it is an aspect of the problem which apparently figures in President Roosevelt's calculations, and it has almost certainly had some influence in setting him against invoking the Neutrality Act. How much influence only he can say.

To most of his advisers at the State Department, it is enough to know that if we don't stop Japan, nobody will. Even if the threat to South America is a myth or a bogey, they would say, we still ought to stop Japan. For if she wins, sooner or later there will be a general war. And sooner or later we'll be drawn into it, try as we may to keep out.

WHAT CAN WE DO?

But what can we *do* to stop Japan?

One thing at least seems clear, and that is this: no amount

of shouting and table-thumping is going to do it. That is the method we have been using ever since 1899. And we have had precious little luck.

THE RECORD

Let's run over the record.

In 1899 Secretary Hay tried to get the western nations to commit themselves to abide by the policy of the "Open Door": they did so only half-heartedly and with numerous reservations.

After the Boxer Rebellion, Hay tried again. This time he expanded the "Open Door" policy to include not only equal trading rights in China but also the defense of her "territorial and administrative integrity." But the only nation which made any binding promise was Japan. And, in the long view of history, that promise has come to seem very much like a deliberate trick.

When Japan was fighting Russia on the plains of Manchuria, the fact that she had promised to respect the "Open Door" policy, and Russia hadn't, made President Theodore Roosevelt use his influence to help Japan win. As soon as she had won, she promptly forgot her promise, and President Roosevelt came to realize that he had been fooled.

For, once she had set her foot on Manchurian soil, Japan began to extend her influence there and crowd China out. In 1910 Japan annexed Korea outright. And her penetration of Manchuria continued unabated.

During the World War, when Japan confronted China with her Twenty-one Demands, which would have reduced China to a Japanese dependency forthwith, we protested, and though our protest helped to check Japan for a time, it did not prevent her from trying later to realize her ambition to master China.

After the World War we again tried to get our policy adopted. And once again we were fooled. Exhausted by the effort of the war, and determined to concentrate their attention on maintaining peace nearer home, the western nations had come to realize that they could no longer afford to maintain in Asia the naval squadrons, the military posts, and the civil authorities required to carry on their former practice of obtaining leaseholds and spheres of influence in China. So, after more than twenty years, they finally agreed to adopt the "Open Door" policy and respect China's independence and territory. In order to get Japan to adopt the policy too, they made a bargain with her: they agreed to limit their navies and refrain from extending their fortifications in the Pacific Ocean. In this agreement we joined. It meant that we were putting Japan on her honor to keep her word, for as long as the naval limitations continued neither we nor any other nation could hope to hold her to it by force or threat of force. But, embodied as it was in a solemn treaty, Japan's promise seemed so good that we were willing to take the chance.

We lost. Just ten years after the promise was renewed, Japan broke it again. Secure in the knowledge that, as a result of our part of the bargain, neither we nor any other nation could stop her single-handed, Japan invaded and captured Manchuria. And our protests—and the protests of the League of Nations—had just about as much influence with her as a letter from a Sunday school teacher would have on a gangster. When she had taken Manchuria, she added Jehol and began nibbling at China proper. Now she has conquered the five provinces of North China, has driven Chiang Kai-shek and the Kuomintang government out of Nanking, and is well on the way toward dominating the whole country. As for the "Open Door," it is closing so fast you can almost feel the draft.

No, all our protests have been little more than a series of humiliating failures. Again and again we have thundered, and again and again we have been tricked or defied. If we are to stop Japan, we shall almost certainly have to try something stronger than words.

SANCTIONS?

What can we try? Sanctions?

As the chart on the next page shows, although Japan raises all her own food, and produces most of her own coal, she is dependent on the outside world for many of her most important raw materials. Doubtless she took care to accumulate reserves of these before she launched her attack on China. If we alone applied an embargo on sales to Japan, she would simply transfer her orders elsewhere. But if the United States, Great Britain, the Netherlands, France and Russia all agreed not to sell to Japan, and kept their agreement long enough, they could cause her a lot of trouble and perhaps stop the progress of her army.

Of course, these countries would have to come to an agreement before sanctions could be applied. And that is where the difficulties begin. France and Britain both have possessions in Eastern Asia, and they are afraid that, if they joined in applying sanctions to Japan, she would retaliate by attacking those possessions. And they are too much concerned about Europe to feel able to spare the ships and men it would take to defend them. They therefore insist that before they can consider sanctions they must get from the United States a hard and fast

85

JAPAN

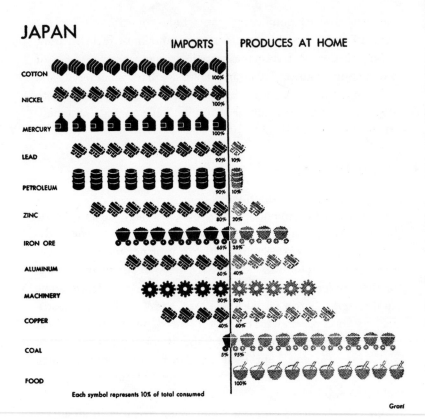

IMPORTS | PRODUCES AT HOME

COTTON — 100%

NICKEL — 100%

MERCURY — 100%

LEAD — 90% | 10%

PETROLEUM — 90% | 10%

ZINC — 80% | 20%

IRON ORE — 65% | 35%

ALUMINUM — 60% | 40%

MACHINERY — 50% | 50%

COPPER — 40% | 60%

COAL — 5% | 95%

FOOD — 100%

Each symbol represents 10% of total consumed

Gront

guarantee to come to their aid in case their Asiatic possessions should be menaced. But for us to give such a promise would mean that we had joined in a defensive alliance, and "entangling alliances" have been contrary to our policy since Washington's Farewell Address. If the State Department should make such an alliance, the Senate, which has the final word about all treaties, would probably repudiate it. But, without it, Britain and France will not even talk about sanctions. And that seems to be that.

86

BOYCOTT?

Since sanctions are apparently "out," at least for the present, what *is* there for us to do? How about boycotting Japan? Wouldn't that stop her?

It might, and it might not. It's hard to say. The last chart shows that Japan sells a good proportion of her exports in the United States. A substantial decline in her sales to us would not only affect her ability to purchase raw materials but would seriously reduce the revenues of her government. It would also increase the poverty of her farmers and industrial workers, who are already finding it very hard to make a living. But whether the ultimate effect of a boycott would be economic·collapse, revolt, or increased support for the militarists is anybody's guess. When sanctions were imposed on Italy, which is almost as vulnerable as Japan, the result was not to stop her invasion of Ethiopia but to rally her people around Mussolini. The same thing might happen in Japan.

FORCE?

But if it is apparently impossible for the great powers to come to an agreement about sanctions, and a privately organized boycott is not certain to be effective, is there no way for us to stop Japan? How about force? Can't we do it that way?

Scarcely, alone. There are 7,000 miles of water between us and Japan, and ever since the Washington Conference she has had a navy which is supreme in her own waters. This means that, by ourselves, we couldn't do very much. In fact, naval experts differ as to whether we could even hold the Philippines if Japan made a real effort to take them. As for collective naval action in cooperation with Great Britain and

France, that is even farther from the realm of possibilities than are sanctions.

This brings us back where we started. Apparently, when you come right down to it, there is very little more we *can* do than we have been doing. And the danger of continuing our present policy is that some incident, or series of incidents, like the bombing of the *Panay*, may drag us into a war we would have very little chance of winning, and almost no chance at all of gaining anything from.

COLLECTIVE ACTION

There are three alternatives to this. Conceivably we could reverse our time-honored stand on alliances and give the British and French the mutual assistance pact they want. Then we could go ahead with them in imposing sanctions on Japan, even in threatening the use of force. In fact, we might even be able to come to an agreement with Britain short of an actual alliance. It would all depend on how solidly we as a nation gave our support to the President and the Secretary of State. As the one thing Japan seems to fear is close cooperation between the United States and Great Britain, even a show of such cooperation might make her think twice. It also might not. It might mean war. And that is a possibility we ought to face squarely if we choose this course.

PEACEFUL CHANGE

The second alternative is the method of "peaceful change."

In common with the other "dissatisfied" nations, Germany and Italy, Japan claims that she has been unfairly deprived of access to markets and raw materials, and that without such access her people cannot continue to prosper and flourish. And,

JAPANESE EXPORTS 1936

TOTAL VALUE

31% TO THE UNITED STATES — 69% TO THE REST OF THE WORLD

Each symbol represents 10% of total exports

VALUE OF PRINCIPAL EXPORTS (AND AMERICA'S SHARE)

 COTTON TISSUES  2.8% OF 483,591 YEN

 RAW SILK 85.0% OF 392,809 YEN

 ARTIFICIAL SILK TISSUES 4% OF 149,170 YEN

 CANNED AND BOTTLED FOOD 21.7% OF 71,077 YEN

 SILK TISSUES 11.1% OF 68,027 YEN

 KNITTED GOODS 13.6% OF 49,988 YEN

 POTTERIES 36.0% OF 43,192 YEN

 VEGETABLE FATTY OILS 87.1% OF 37,308 YEN

 TOYS 37.5% OF 36,459 YEN

GLASS 11.9% OF 25,627 YEN

Each disc represents 25,000 yen worth of exports
Black indicates share to the United States

Grant

to a very large extent, this is true. Nations *do* discriminate against both the buyers and the sellers of other nations. They employ export duties to prevent large quantities of their available supplies of raw materials from passing into the hands of other, and perhaps not very friendly, states. And they erect high tariff walls to keep the products of other states out of their "protected" markets. Sometimes they even resort to the "quota" system to hold exports down. Or they pass such strict regulations about "foreign exchange" that it is difficult for their citizens to buy anything abroad.

Now both Italy and Japan have attempted to justify their recent war-making by saying that the other nations of the world have left them no other way of obtaining access to sources of raw materials for their industries, or markets for their goods. And Germany is threatening to use force if necessary to get her pre-war colonies back. For this reason it has been suggested that, if the nations of the world could only sit down in a conference and agree on means to provide such access, one of the major causes of, or excuses for, war would be removed. The conference would have to find ways to lower or abolish export duties, or at least see that they did not *discriminate* between buyers. It would have to reach an agreement to lower tariff barriers and abolish preferential trade agreements and other obstacles to international trade. It would probably have to seek and find means of stabilizing currencies.

Perhaps it would even have to go into such knotty questions as living standards, for these too have their bearing on international trade. And it would almost certainly have to tackle the knotty problems of disarmament or the limitation of armaments by mutual agreement, for one of the reasons why nations are striving to make themselves "self-sufficient" today is the possibility of finding themselves unable to wage war successfully if they aren't. The task of such a conference would be tremendously difficult, and some people think it could never be done. But if it is not done, the world seems likely to become involved sooner or later in a war still more devastating and still more horrible than the World War. And many sober people wonder how much of human civilization would be left if such a war should come.

What this proposal really amounts to is holding the peace conference *before* the general war begins instead of after it is over. To such a conference the United States would have much to contribute. We might take the lead in calling it. In fact, in our reciprocal trade agreements, we have already pointed the way, for these agreements attempt to do on a small scale what the conference would do on a world-wide scale. By lowering our tariffs, we could offer large markets to the "dissatisfied" nations. We could lend aid in a program to stabilize currencies. We could use some of our extensive capital resources to help develop the backward areas of the world, and in other ways to adjust economic inequalities. In the case of Japan, we could repeal our Immigration Act of 1924 and thus remove one more cause of the resentment the "have-not" countries feel for the "haves."

Of course, there's a catch in this "peaceful change" idea, too. Suppose we should go ahead, hold the conference, make the offers. What's to prevent Italy, Germany and Japan from accepting everything we and the other nations are willing to grant them *and then* taking whatever else they want by force anyway? Maybe such concessions as the advocates of "peaceful change" propose would only whet the appetites of the "have-not" nations for more. If that should turn out to be the case, we might find that we had unwittingly brought the world still nearer the brink of large-scale war by strengthening the very nations which apparently stand to gain from it.

ISOLATION

If we find we can't reverse our policy on alliances and join in an effort to stop Japan by force or threat of force, and if we can't see our way clear to some such grand-scale readjustment as that suggested above, a third alternative to staying in range of the shooting still remains to us: we can invoke our Neutrality Act and get out. You have already seen what the objections to such a course are. It means a clean break with a tradition now nearly forty years old. It means the loss of much of our nation's prestige. It means the end of our influence in world affairs. It may even mean the triumph of Italy, Germany and Japan, and an eventual united drive by all three in South America.

But, theoretically at least, to choose this course should also mean that we could reduce our expenditures on the navy by perhaps as much as half a billion dollars a year, for it is no secret that the greater part of our navy is designed primarily for possible action in the Far East. It should mean that, for the present, and perhaps for a long time to come, we could concentrate on improving conditions at home, and stop worrying about events on the other side of the world. Most important of all, it should mean the end of any immediate danger of our becoming involved in war—unless, of course, the so-called "fascist" powers should take our withdrawal from the Far East as a sign of weakness and should launch a general war of conquest forthwith.

Some people think that the objections to withdrawing from China now are so serious that we can't even consider it. Presi-

92

dent Roosevelt and the State Department apparently hold this view. Others, including a considerable number of Senators and Congressmen, believe that we should put our own immediate security above everything else and get out, now, before it is too late.

Most of those who hold this latter view are inclined to scoff at the argument that, after conquering China, Japan will threaten us in our own bailiwick. Some of them say that Japan will get so badly bogged down in China that she will not be able to give her attention to more distant spoils for many years to come. Others scout the whole idea of a German-Italian-Japanese threat to South America. All agree that, *if* Japan should come our way, we would be in a much better position to oppose her successfully here than we should be in China. Even if Japan should succeed in establishing her sway over China, and should then join Germany and Italy in a general war, these people think, we'd stand a better chance of keeping clear of it if we get out of China now than if we don't.

AMERICA'S CHOICE

Between these three alternatives, then, our choice seems to lie. For, difficult and uncertain though they all are, any one of them seems to make more sense than our present Far Eastern policy. Produced by an intermittent tug-of-war between the President and the State Department on one side and a majority of Senators and Congressmen, backed by a good proportion of the voters, on the other, our present policy often succeeds in achieving nothing but failure, as at Brussels. It does not do very much to preserve world peace; still less does it succeed in saving the "territorial and administrative integrity" of China. In fact, it doesn't even serve to keep the "Open Door"

93

open. About all it does is to cost us a great deal of money—one authority estimates $600,000,000 a year, over twice as much as all our investors and business men together get out of China. It obliges us to keep up a much larger navy than we shall probably ever need to defend our own borders. And it leaves us in a position where, sooner or later, some "incident," or series of incidents, like the sinking of the *Panay*, may drag us into a war we could scarcely hope to wage successfully and from which we would have far less to gain than to lose.

SUGGESTED READING

Bisson, T. A., and Goslin, Ryllis Alexander. *Clash in the Pacific.* Headline Book No. 5. New York. Foreign Policy Association. 1936.

Goslin, Ryllis Alexander, and Stone, William T. *America Contradicts Herself: The Story of Our Foreign Policy.* Headline Book No. 7. New York. Foreign Policy Association. 1936.

Stone, William T., and Eichelberger, Clark M. *Peaceful Change—The Alternative to War.* Headline Book No. 12. New York. Foreign Policy Association. 1937.

Bisson, T. A. "American Policy in the Far East." *Foreign Policy Reports.* February 1, 1937. New York. Foreign Policy Association.

DeWilde, John C. "Can Japan Be Quarantined?" *Foreign Policy Reports,* December 1, 1937. New York. Foreign Policy Association.

Lasker, Bruno. *Japan in Jeopardy.* New York. Institute of Pacific Relations. 1937.

Field, Frederick V. *China's Capacity for Resistance.* New York. Institute of Pacific Relations. 1937.

Lockwood, William W., Jr. *America and the Far Eastern War.* New York. Institute of Pacific Relations. 1937.

Dulles, Foster Rhea. *Forty Years of American-Japanese Re-'ations.* New York. Appleton-Century. 1937.

Morse, Hosea B., and McNair, Harley F. *Far Eastern International Relations.* Boston. Houghton Mifflin. 1931.

Vinacke, Harold M. *A History of the Far East in Modern Times.* New York. Crofts. 1936.

Bemis, Samuel F. *A Diplomatic History of the United States.* New York. Holt. 1936.

A NOTE ON HEADLINE BOOKS

War in China is one of the Foreign Policy Association's HEAD-LINE BOOKS. The object of the series is to provide sufficient unbiased background information to enable readers to reach intelligent and independent conclusions on the important international problems of the day. HEADLINE BOOKS are prepared under the supervision of the Department of Popular Education of the Foreign Policy Association with the cooperation of the Association's Research Staff of experts.

The Foreign Policy Association is a non-profit American organization founded "to carry on research and educational activities to aid in the understanding and constructive development of American foreign policy." It is an impartial research organization and does not seek to promote any one point of view toward international affairs. Such views as may be expressed or implied in any of its publications are those of the author and not of the Association.

For further information about HEADLINE BOOKS and the other publications of the Foreign Policy Association, write to the Department of Popular Education, Foreign Policy Association, 8 West 40th Street, New York, N. Y.